Minnesota Collects

Minnesota Collects

TEXT BY JACK EL-HAI

ARTIFACT PHOTOGRAPHY BY ERIC MORTENSON

RESEARCH ASSISTANCE BY THE COLLECTIONS STAFF
OF THE MINNESOTA HISTORICAL SOCIETY

Minnesota Historical Society Press   St. Paul

Front cover: Cootie toy made by a Plymouth firm, about 1980; volume of reminiscences and drawings by the Frances Haynes James family of St. Paul, 1902–15; cast-metal piano lamp, late 1920s or 1930s. *Back cover:* Horse bog shoes made by an Isanti County farmer; automobile built by Ole Bjella of McIntosh, 1906; Ojibway *makak* or container from the first half of the twentieth century; Toastmaster pop-up toaster made by a Minneapolis firm, about 1930; photograph of Esther Lagerstedt, taken in Stillwater about 1890 and shown in a cabinet-card picture frame from the same period.

Frontispiece: The Minnesota Historical Society holds the nation's largest collection of materials relating to railroad history. Among them are the corporate records of the Great Northern, Northern Pacific, and Soo Line railroads and their subsidiaries—more than fifteen thousand cubic feet of correspondence, minute books, financial and legal records, mechanical drawings, and advertisements. Artifact materials range from locomotives to train models, signal lanterns, oilcans, promotional mementos, and depot signs.

Production of this book was supported by the Minnesota Historical Society's North Star Heritage Fund, by a grant from the George A. MacPherson Fund, St. Paul, and by a gift given in memory of Arnold E. Anderson, book lover, Mahtomedi, Minnesota.

Minnesota Historical Society Press
St. Paul 55102

Printed in Canada
10 9 8 7 6 5 4 3 2 1

This publication is printed on a coated paper manufactured on an acid-free base to ensure its long life.

Library of Congress
Cataloging-in-Publication Data
El-Hai, Jack.
    Minnesota collects / text by Jack El-Hai.
        p.   cm.
    ISBN 0-87351-279-0 (cloth) —
    ISBN 0-87351-280-4 (paper)
        1. Minnesota—History—Pictorial works.
2. Material culture—Minnesota—Pictorial works.
3. Minnesota—History. 4. Minnesota
Historical Society—Pictorial works. I. Title.
F607.E4 1992   92-18368
977.6—dc20

Contents

Perspectives on Our Past:
Introducing the Collections of the
Minnesota Historical Society

People in Minnesota treasure their history, and they record it in many ways. Long before the state was formed, the first inhabitants carved images of hunters, thunderbirds, and other powerful symbols on rock faces emerging from the prairie landscape. Centuries later, immigrants and their children came to value the ordinary objects that carried the memories of long years of building up a homestead. Minnesotans chronicle their lives and work in diaries and letters, in artworks, in documents from business and government, and in countless unique and everyday things.

This book presents a glimpse into the vast collections held by the Minnesota Historical Society, which has gathered and preserved materials relating to regional history and made them available to the public since 1849. With the opening of the History Center in 1992, the Society is at last able to bring these collections together in one building for use by everyone and for safe storage.

We think that you will be surprised at the variety of objects and documents appearing on the following pages. They range in size from a locomotive to a campaign button, in purpose from a railroad's corporate records to a child's homemade top. They are as old as a granite tool used nine thousand years ago, as new as a poster for a Prince movie. They are papers and books, farm machinery, paintings and sculptures, clothes, photographs, maps, tools, ice skates, war souvenirs, and many other media through which history is captured.

Minnesotans took the first official steps to preserve their heritage in 1849, the year the territory was founded. Enthusiastic about the land to which they had committed their futures, they established the Minnesota Historical Society during the first session of the territorial legislature. The Society's purpose was to collect and preserve "publications, manuscripts, antiquities, curiosities, and all other things pertaining to the social, political and natural history of Minnesota."

This broad charter has allowed the Society to grow from generation to generation, adding new programs as it discovers new ways to fulfill its mission. Some programs have been strong from the earliest years. Publishing began in 1850 with the first *Annals of the Minnesota Historical Society;*

two years later a landmark Dakota-language dictionary was published in cooperation with the Smith-sonian Institution. The library also flourished, numbering 56,000 books and pamphlets by the turn of the century. Minnesota's newspapers – described by Governor Alexander Ramsey in 1849 as the "day-books of history" – have been collected by the Society from the dates of their first publication, thereby safeguarding an invaluable record of the region's development.

Other programs achieved prominence as the state grew. Beginning in the 1890s, leading citizens like Henry H. Sibley and their families gave the Society letters and papers representing decades of political and business activity since the 1830s. As they became established, corporations, labor unions, churches, and associations of every kind also recognized the importance of preserving their records. In 1922, when the St. Louis County Historical Society was founded, the Minnesota Historical Society began a program of working with counties to preserve local history; by the 1940s all of Minnesota's counties had formed their own associations. In the 1960s and 1970s, public enthusiasm for exploring the past led to a statewide historic sites program based on the concept of learning in the place where history happened. The state of Minnesota transferred its archives to the Society in 1971, bringing a flow of documents that has expanded as government tasks and paperwork have grown. Education, which underlies all of the institution's work, has generated activities as diverse as tours, public pro-grams, and radio broadcasts. Today the Society works closely with the schools in the teaching of state history, including an innovative curriculum for students in the fifth through seventh grades.

Minnesotans also recover the details and spirit of their history through objects that they have used, saved, and given to the Society. The museum began with items that were collected and displayed for their interest as curiosities; when fire destroyed many of these items in 1881, the losses included objects "illustrating domestic life in Polynesia." Collecting policy shifted over the years, and today's collections reflect more than a century of acquiring and preserving objects related to state history. Strengths include household and decorative items, clothing and textiles, arts and crafts, cor-porate collections, archaeological artifacts, and Dakota and Ojibway cultural materials. Archaeologists and other researchers working since the 1930s have succeeded in recovering artifacts from the region's earliest cross-cultural economic enterprise – the fur trade, which spanned the centuries between 1600 and 1850. In the 1980s the Society began an aggressive effort to collect twentieth-century materials documenting the lives of workers, artisans, women, families, and ethnic groups.

By 1992 the Society held in trust for the people of Minnesota some 550,000 books, 37,000 maps, 250,000 cataloged photographs, 5,500 artworks, 1,650 oral history interviews, 4.5 million newspaper issues, 38,000 cubic feet of manuscripts, 45,000 cubic feet of government records, 165,000 museum objects, and nearly 800,000 archaeological artifacts. Clearly, the hardest part of producing this book has been the task of selecting a few things to represent the breadth and depth of this tangible heritage.

Minnesota Collects reveals the private stories, as well as the public ones, contained in that heritage. Some of the stories are told in pictures, and others unfold through the words of people who left accounts of their lives, emotions, and opinions. Together these stories bring the larger aspects of the state's history into view — life in small towns, the world of work, the experience of growing up, and many others. The stories enlighten and entertain.

In bringing so many objects and documents together to tell these stories, we hope to show that history can be approached in sometimes unexpected ways. For example, a visitor to the Oliver H. Kelley Farm — the nineteenth-century farmstead operated by the Society near Elk River — might see a fanning mill resembling one used years ago on his or her family farm to separate grain from weed seeds and chaff. Inside the Kelley home, the visitor might watch a guide prepare vegetables grown from seeds of the same historic varieties produced more than a hundred years ago. From these beginnings, a researcher who seeks to know more about changes in farm life can turn to a wealth of three-dimensional and documentary materials. Artifacts, from tractors and hand-crafted tools to corn planters and seed company displays, enlarge our knowledge about farming over the years. As we learn how to "read" the object, it reveals much about its purpose and times. Photographs since the 1880s depict the methods that Minnesota farmers used in different eras. Documents include letters and diaries written by farm families from territorial days to the present, as well as books, magazines, catalogs, and the records of the Minnesota Department of Agriculture. Artists have left their distinctive visions of the land and its cultivation in paintings, prints, and drawings. Oral history keeps the story current, as in interviews that describe changes in the farm economy during the 1980s.

This example represents only one of many possibilities for exploring our past through the collections of the Minnesota Historical Society. Some of the approaches are familiar, as when an enthusiast about family history finds links to earlier generations in census records and old newspapers. But other links are present in the objects and documents — artifacts, photographs, maps, oral histories — that expand our understanding of the world in which those generations lived.

On behalf of the Society's staff members, especially those who prepared this book (their names are listed on page 118), I invite you to participate in the collections as a user, a donor, or a visitor to our exhibitions. The History Center in St. Paul now provides convenient access to all the collections — books, manuscripts and archives, photographs, and museum and archaeological artifacts — within a single research center. Collections are also exhibited at the History Center, at the historic sites, and in traveling exhibits.

We encourage you to see this book as an offering of possibilities, of creative ways to uncover the past and to look at the present. The collections of the Minnesota Historical Society form an interrelated whole, and one that is always in the process of growth and change. "Write your history as you go along," urged historian Edward D. Neill at the first annual meeting of the Society in 1850. His advice challenges us to examine our own times to see how our lives are reflected in things that are rare and valuable (a supercomputer manufactured in Minnesota) as well as commonplace (a lawn sign from a school board election). Tomorrow's collections are created through the perceptions and actions of people who continue to understand the importance of this shared legacy.

Nina M. Archabal, Director

On the Streets of Small Towns

MAIN STREET

Carol Kennicott's first view, from her railroad car, of Gopher Prairie, Minnesota — the small town she has moved to from St. Paul, in the company of her new husband — is a crashing moment in Sinclair Lewis's novel, *Main Street*:

> *The huddled low wooden houses broke the plains scarcely more than would a hazel thicket. The fields swept up to it, past it. It was unprotected and unprotecting; there was no dignity in it nor any hope of greatness. Only the tall red grain-elevator and a few tinny church-steeples rose from the mass. It was a frontier camp. It was not a place to live in, not possibly, not conceivably.*

All at once, Carol's city-bred notions of civilization and her illusions about village life deflate. Where she hoped to find the sparkling Twin Cities in miniature, she sees materialism and bleakness in frightening magnification.

In 1921, the year in which *Main Street* went through its twenty-fifth hard-cover printing in twelve months and was shortsightedly stripped of the Pulitzer Prize by the trustees of Columbia University, thousands of Minnesotans and a million readers nationwide assumed that Lewis had based the stultifying town of his tale on his own birthplace: Sauk Centre, Minnesota. "The story would be the same in Ohio or Montana, in Kansas or Kentucky or Illinois," Lewis protested, "and not very differently would it be told Up York State or in the Carolina hills."

The residents of Sauk Centre listened with anger, and for good reason. Not all small towns around the country were alike. Even within Minnesota, a full spectrum of towns filled the map, from mining settlements on the Iron Range to river towns in the southeast. Finally, was it fair to apply big-city standards to a place that was not a city — a kind of place that had a rich life unique to itself? (Certainly, Lewis could answer. He was writing fiction, not history.)

Small-town life, in fact, was far from obsolescent or unpopular in the 1920s. In the first year of that decade there were 624 incorporated towns in Minnesota, an increase of 64 percent since 1900. Many Minnesotans viewed town life as the perfect compromise between the isolation of rural existence and the noisiness of the city.

For seven decades, planning and platting towns had been one of the most common commercial activities in Minnesota — usually spurred by a speculator's desire to make money in real estate. The site of the village and its purpose, however, varied regionally within the state.

In southeastern Minnesota, the demand for river landings inspired the platting of settlements. In the western part, the expansion of railroads sparked the germination of towns. The construction of a rail line gave farmers a way to reach grain markets and brought the need for the agricultural support services (depots, elevators, equipment dealers, dry goods stores) that a town could provide.

But by the arrival of the 1920s, most river towns and farming communities had already been established. Many of the new towns launched during the second decade of the century were located in the north, settlements that owed their existence to nearby mining operations. Often mining companies themselves planned town sites — or abruptly forced them to move when they discovered valuable mineral deposits beneath the streets and homes, as happened with Hibbing beginning in 1919.

Whatever their origins, Minnesota's towns in the 1920s boasted a flavorful commercial and social life. The fictional Main Street that Sinclair Lewis mocked for its petty boosterism provided, in its real-life versions, an impressive variety of goods and services. Although very small towns with fewer than 250 people might have little more than a grain elevator, fueling pump, and church, larger places contained full business districts: movie theaters, department stores, druggists, dressmakers, studio photographers, hardware stores, saloons, power stations, courthouses, and libraries.

In many communities the social life centered on churches and synagogues, a fact well known to the railroad companies that donated town lots to congregations interested in building houses of worship. Spires rising above the trees, like the ever-present water tower, gave the town a visual identity. But the religious centers offered much more than just a pretty steeple; they provided a home for group worship, kids' religious-education classes, and social activities that held fast the social fabric of many towns.

And that solid sense of community — sometimes welcoming, sometimes oppressive — is what people most remember about the small-town experience. How we react to it depends on whether we are like Carol Kennicott or the less dreamy boosters of Main Street.

◄

RAILWAY STATIONS

A 1960 wall map of the Northern Pacific Railway system forms the backdrop for photographs taken in 1906–07 of the Great Northern Railway stations in Alexandria, Wayzata, and Barnesville.

In Lewis's *Main Street,* Carol Kennicott believes she instantly reads the complexion of a town in the view through the window of her stationary train: "The station agent hoisted a dead calf aboard the baggage-car. There were no other visible activities in Schoenstrom. In the quiet of the halt, Carol could hear a horse kicking his stall, a carpenter shingling a roof. . . . The railroad station was a one-room frame box, a mirey cattle-pen on one side and a crimson wheat-elevator on the other."

SINCLAIR LEWIS
The author inscribed a page of his first published novel, *Our Mr. Wrenn*.

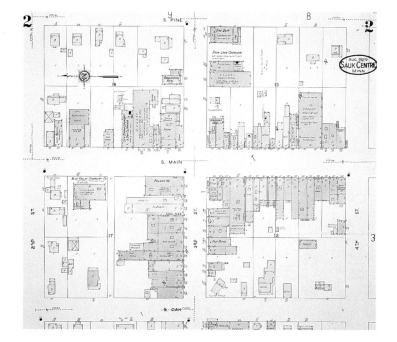

SAUK CENTRE
Sauk Centre's Main Street in 1929, less than a decade after Sinclair Lewis's novel was published, shown on an insurance map

◄

SMALL TOWN ARTIFACTS

If you could reduce a Minnesota town to a paper essence, you might find yourself with a pile of postcards, milk bottle tops, and bank notes.

Commercial postcards – like the 1908 view of Cold Spring at top right on this page – are often our only record of the way a town looked in its early days. And in that town the creamery was likely to be one of the most important local businesses. A chemist with the Minnesota Department of Agriculture collected these chocolate-milk bottle tops, all dating before 1965, in the course of his inspection duties. Creameries first began manufacturing chocolate milk in 1919.

The bank notes were among those issued by hundreds of Minnesota banks between 1863 and 1935 under the National Banking Act, which established a banking network to replace an unsound state bank system. The notes were usually printed in Washington, D.C., and shipped to the banks for distribution. They typically contained such information as the date issued, the bank serial number, the signatures of bank officers, and a denomination ranging from $1 to $1,000.

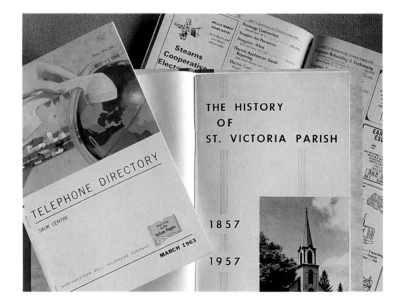

PHONES AND CHURCHES

The church, a spiritual institution, and the telephone, a technological innovation, have each played important roles in the social lives of towns. Church histories and local telephone directories are a rich source of information about a town's earlier days.

MEDICINE WAGON

During the 1890s Dr. Peter Mark, a patent medicine manufacturer who lived in the Polk County town of Fosston, used this wagon (pictured with a detail of its rear door) to peddle and deliver his goods. Mark's medicines included "Lung Balsam (with Tar)" and "Gall Cure for Horses, etc."

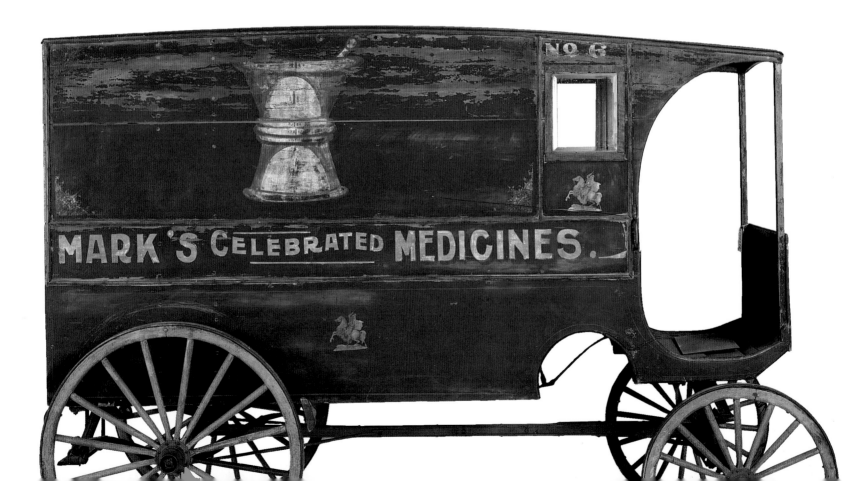

JEWEL ROBBERY

Perham, in Otter Tail County, is the setting for *The Great Perham Jewel Robbery,* an amateur production by Bernard Kemper. In the 1930s he filmed family and friends acting out scenes inspired by the fare at the local movie theater.

FILM PROJECTOR

In the early 1940s the attic of the Strand Theater in Princeton yielded a treasure: a hand-cranked Victor Animatograph movie projector. About twenty-five years earlier the projector had probably toured the Princeton area for tent film screenings.

THEATER PROGRAM

Many Main Streets had cinemas, and the movies did make it there – though perhaps later than they were screened in the cities.

PHOTOGRAPHERS

The constant flow of family, social, and business activity made small towns a fertile place for photographers, both professionals and amateurs. John Runk, based in Stillwater, took thousands of photos during a professional career that stretched from the turn of the century through the 1960s. A spectacular example is his picture of the collapse of P. N. Peterson's Granite Company building in Stillwater during a fire in 1909. Joseph J. Brechet of Glencoe, the owner of a dry goods store, took his photographs avocationally. Snapped around 1900, his photo shows his daughter Bertha Brechet hamming it up with one of her father's newspaper ads.

BACK PORCH

Henry Clay Bull, a Wright County land speculator and the organizer of a successful grain elevator, a creamery, and a canning firm, built a two-and-a-half-story house at the corner of Third Street and Moors Avenue in Cokato in 1878. The servants entered the house through this back porch (shown with detail), which was saved when the structure was razed a century after it was erected.

The Great Outdoors

A SET OF TWELVE DIFFERENT STAMPS SENT FOR 4/

EVINRUDING FOR THE FISHERMEN

EVINRUDE MOTOR COMPANY, MILWAUKEE

WHERE THE RIVER BEGINS

Today Lake Itasca, the source of the Mississippi River, lies entirely within the thirty-two thousand acres of Itasca State Park. During autumn bicyclists pedal along the park's paved roads and admire the glorious color of the foliage. Visitors can drive in and park within one hundred yards of the headwaters. To the right of the trail leading to the lake are restrooms and an air-cooled gift shop. The soles of millions of shoes have ground fine the surface of the trail itself, and hikers following it can stop along the way to read historical markers that mention names like Pike and Schoolcraft.

The trail abruptly ends at a scattering of slippery rocks that spans the river at its source. This is the place kids dream about, that Robert Ripley wrote about in "Believe It or Not," that tourism brochures mention as a highlight of a Minnesota visit. Access to the Mississippi headwaters— indeed, to everything outdoors that is contained within Minnesota's scores of state, county, city, and national parks and forests—seems easy, attainable to anyone who really wants to make the trip.

The Mississippi headwaters, however, is also a place hidden in the deep woods of years past that obsessed Europeans and their American descendants. Located in a region not highly valued strategically or economically, it resisted their search for the better part of two centuries. Nowadays, you can drive there within a few hours from virtually any part of Minnesota.

The parade of headwaters seekers began perhaps as early as the 1620s, when Samuel de Champlain, the governor of New France and founder of the colony of Quebec, caught word of a great river west of his territory. A half-century later, when Louis Jolliet arrived in present-day Minnesota, he became the first European known to have set eyes on the state's most prominent natural feature, the Mississippi River.

Among the earliest of the Europeans to travel a substantial distance upriver along the Mississippi was Pierre Charles Le Sueur, a Frenchman who had experience trading with the Dakota people and peddling beaver skins from the Lake Superior region. In 1700 his party boated from the river's mouth in the Gulf of Mexico all the way north to the Falls of St. Anthony before veering west along the Minnesota River.

Sixty-seven years later Jonathan Carver, a Massachusetts-born officer in the British army who was in search of a northwest passage to the Pacific Ocean, led another push up the waterway. But his group angled northeast to Lake Superior before turning back. Carver, however, was the first explorer to draw a picture of the falls, and his illustration fired the imagination of those who followed.

Others who hunted for the river's source bore the credentials of the young United States government. One was Lt. Zebulon Montgomery Pike of the U.S. Army, who was instructed to learn about the Indians of Minnesota, to discover who else was living in the region, and to find out about the fur trade. He incorrectly identified Leech and Cass lakes as the sources. In 1823 Giacomo Costantino Beltrami, an Italian adventurer, erroneously picked Lake Julia as the site of the headwaters.

Another, ultimately successful, was Henry Rowe Schoolcraft. A writer and mineral expert, he investigated Pike's claimed headwaters in 1820. A dozen years later, guided by an Ojibway named Ozawindib (Yellow Head), Schoolcraft identified a nearby smaller lake that truly supplied the river with its earliest waters. Combining the Latin words *veritas* and *caput* (meaning "true head"), he named the lake Itasca.

Most of the Mississippi explorers undertook their journeys for economic gain – to find a direct route to the Pacific, to speed the fur trade, or to reach trading partners in the interior. Into the twentieth century, in fact, Minnesotans tended to look at the outdoors simply as a big warehouse of natural resources: lumber, minerals, and game. Around the 1920s, however, with the depletion of the forests, a change was in the making. Recreation, not exploitation, emerged as the most popular reason to appreciate Minnesota's outdoor world.

◄

CAMP BED

Recreational camping rose in popularity during the 1920s when the Minnesota state government aggressively began acquiring park land. Typical of the period's bulky outdoor furniture is this folding bed, constructed by the Minneapolis Bedding Company. Vacationers probably used such equipment for cabin furnishings as well as for camping.

On the bed is a book by naturalist Sigurd F. Olson and part of a portable mess kit used by a fire-detail team of the U.S. Forest Service around 1930. Along with a tent, a cooking pot, and food, the kit was a necessity for the twenty-five-worker crews.

FALLS OF ST. ANTHONY
The engraving from a drawing by
Jonathan Carver, published in his 1781
*Travels through the Interior Parts of North
America*

DAGUERREOTYPES
Minnesota's earliest photographers,
the daguerreotypists, were attracted to
the Falls of St. Anthony in the 1850s
and made it one of the first landscapes
in the region to be recorded by camera.

CASS LAKE FISHING

Zebulon Pike mistook Cass Lake for a source of the Mississippi River, but Minnesotans of later generations took advantage of it – and thousands of other state lakes – as a source of family recreation, fishing, and resort-business income. In the 1920s the resorts in the central lake district were flourishing and their brochures and postcards included pictures that dominated the popular image of Minnesota for decades: fish, summer cottages, wood-paneled lodge interiors, and thick forests. Fishing was the main activity at these resorts, and the development of lures and decoys to catch unwary fish received much creative attention.

DUCK BOAT
Parkers Prairie Boat Works built this
all-wood duck boat in the early 1930s.

IS THE WINTER WEATHER DEADLY . . .

In the spring of 1906 a schoolteacher named Annie Shelland Williams was offered a position at a new school in the town of Northome in Koochiching County. She accepted the job only reluctantly. During the previous fall her hired helper, Van, had threatened to contest her claim for her homestead near Little Fork if she remained away longer than six months. That land, upon which she lived in a small cabin, meant everything to Annie. "I learned to row a boat, paddle a canoe and walk ten miles at one stretch," she wrote in her reminiscences. "All this because of my homestead. . . . It was God's gift and I would keep it."

In the summer Annie set off for Northome, knowing she had to be back at her homestead by January 1, 1907, to thwart Van's threat. She finished the term and began her journey home a few days before Christmas — normally a one-day trip. But the weather was treacherous. "There was no hard freezing but much snow," Annie recalled, "which made the trails impossible and swamps and sink holes were flooded." The stage was unable to make the run from the train station in Big Falls to Little Fork.

Determined not to miss her deadline, Annie decided to ignore the risky weather and walk home from Big Falls. She found a man named St. Syre to guide her through the woods. In her reminiscences she described their dangerous hike with St. Syre leading the way:

> We broke through the thin ice on the first swale and our boots
> became wet. . . . After we had traveled some time, the glare
> on the white snow and the monotanous [sic] rise and fall of

his black [bootheels] bothered me. . . . Suddenly I could see nothing. Every thing was black.

> I cried aloud. He turned[,] listened to my tale of woe and said, "Snow blindness. We will stop right here after I take off my mackinaw and will have some tea. You close your eyes and rest."
>
> . . . He let me sleep some time before he awakened me. As I came to, I shouted, "Thank God, I can see again. . . ."
>
> "The sun is going down," he remarked, "we better get moving."
>
> He started. I tried to but my knees refused to act. I could not lift my feet. Finally, in sheer desperation, I turned up my [skirt], took hold of my heavy woolen stockings and pulled. My knees moved slightly. Again and again I pulled until my muscles obeyed me and I could lift my feet as usual. When I got in motion I dared not stop.

After still more hardship, Annie made it back to her homestead and immediately slept for eighteen hours. As she slept the hard freeze arrived, sending temperatures down to forty degrees below zero. "I was sure I had saved my homestead," she wrote.

ICE-FISHING HOUSE

In 1981, at the age of twenty, Mark Heimer of St. Paul built this ice-fishing shack. During its wintertime use Heimer kept inside it two well-worn car seats, a wood-burning stove, and artwork that he painted on the walls to stave off boredom when the fish were not biting. The shack is fully carpeted.

. . . OR A LIFE SAVER?

In his book *Minnesota: Its Character and Climate*, published in 1871, state promoter Ledyard Bill argued that the severe winter weather was an elixir for Minnesotans:

> The atmosphere in Minnesota in the winter is like a wine, so exhilarating is its effects on the system; while its extreme dryness and elasticity prevents any discomfort from the cold which is such a bugbear to many. The extreme cold does not last but for a few days. . . . Why, laboring men in the lumber districts to the north of St. Paul perform their work without overcoats, and frequently, and indeed commonly, without a coat of any kind, simply in their shirt-sleeves. . . .
>
> . . . The snow accumulates gradually, falling in the finest of flakes, and light as down itself. . . . [T]he deerskin moccasins, which many persons habitually wear, are scarcely moistened the season through. . . . The whole winter is a radiant and joyous band of sunny days and starlight nights.

JACK PINE SAVAGE

Except for the nails that form the stubble, the sculpture *Jack Pine Savage* by St. Paul artist John Cisney is made entirely of wood—an appropriate medium for depicting an earthy recluse. "The kind of person who lives in Minnesota's backwoods and prefers to commune with nature," Cisney has called him. "He seldom talks with people and fades into the background when they approach. He cuts wood for a living and lives in an isolated cabin. He might even smell bad."

◄

POWER LINE DISPUTE

In 1973 a proposed electric power line stretching 430 miles from North Dakota to the Twin Cities sparked one of Minnesota's most bitterly fought environmental battles of the twentieth century. Worried about the potential dangers of high-voltage cables crossing their land, farmers and other activists squared off—in physical confrontations and in court—against the electric utility co-ops planning the project. After years of litigation the power line was built. The history of the dispute was recorded in oral history interviews with participants.

THE BIRDS OF MINNESOTA

As a nineteenth-century Minneapolis teenager, Thomas Sadler Roberts filled his bedroom with six hundred stuffed birds and bird skins, a collection of nests and eggs, and other assorted biological specimens. His interests changed little in adulthood. First a physician, later an ornithologist, he published his mammoth study *The Birds of Minnesota* in 1932 at the age of seventy-four. It drew upon notes he had begun compiling in the 1870s, and its seven hundred pictures included the work of some of the century's finest bird artists, such as the naturalist Louis Agassiz Fuertes, whose illustration is shown here.

◄

HEADWATERS MARKER
The message on the headwaters marker is familiar to anyone who has visited the source of the Mississippi River. Successive signs have greeted countless Lake Itasca visitors, including these from the 1940s (far left); the other view appeared on a postcard in the 1920s. Carved out of a partial tree trunk, the marker leaves little doubt of the importance of the headwaters site.

THROUGH THE BIRCHES
Although poorly represented in major art museums and galleries, wildlife art may well have the largest following of any style of painting – and Minnesota has contributed more than its share of successful practitioners. This painting was done about 1960 by Walter J. Wilwerding, one of the state's world-renowned wildlife artists.

EATING OUT
This dinner plate and menu holder were used at Douglas Lodge in Itasca State Park, near the headwaters. The pink flower is the showy lady slipper, the state flower. The placemat comes from the Edgewater Inn on the North Shore of Lake Superior.

NORTH SHORE

Brainerd Childs, photographer from Michigan, sailed the *Wanderer* along the North Shore of Lake Superior in the 1870s to create dramatic and unusual images to sell as stereographs of Minnesota scenery.

WINTER SCENE

Shot for brochures, calendars, and wall decor, the outdoor photos of the Norton & Peel studio convey the image of a clean, pristine, and lush wilderness.

FOREST SERVICE TRUCK

Somehow, from 1911 to 1923 the Minnesota Forest Service maintained thirty-five million acres of land without owning any kind of motorized transportation. In 1923 the agency caved in and purchased this truck (secondhand – it was a four-year-old Ford Model T roadster) for use in the Park Rapids area. The Forest Service retired the truck from active service after three decades, but the vehicle remained on call as a parade truck until 1976. It is now on display at the Forest History Center near Grand Rapids.

The First People

PICTURES ON THE ROCK

In Cottonwood County in southwestern Minnesota, among the cacti, pasque flowers, and thin stalks of wheatgrass, are hunters, thunderbirds, spears in flight, harpoons, men with earspools, shamans, and groups of stickmen carrying spears. There are about two thousand carvings at the Jeffers Petroglyphs site, the state's best-preserved collection of Indian rock carvings.

Before Europeans arrived in America, several other collections of petroglyphic carvings appeared on rock faces around the land that would become Minnesota: for example, below Dayton's Bluff in St. Paul, on an island in Nett Lake in Koochiching County, in Reno Cave in Houston County, and on a bluff site near Stillwater. Except for the Jeffers and Nett Lake sites, almost all of the carvings have since been demolished or vandalized.

Two groups of artists probably carved the graceful figures at Jeffers. The earliest lived as long as 5,000 years ago (during what archaeologists refer to as the Late Archaic period). It is not known whether the Indians who have lived in the region in more recent times are their descendants. The second group most likely left its carvings in the rock between 250 and 1,100 years ago (the Late Woodland period). These carvers probably belonged to the Oto, Iowa, and Yankton Dakota tribes.

Scattered in 218 different clusters, the petroglyphs show a wealth of subjects and aspects of early Indian life. Many depict animals and atlatls (hand-held throwing sticks that allowed hunters to throw spears harder and farther), and these may have been carved as part of the practice of hunting magic. Other images in the rock — shamans and thunderbirds — may have held religious meaning. And some petroglyphs, especially those showing leaders, warriors, and records of bison hunts, may have served as historical chronicles of the lives of people in the tribe.

We do not know how the Dakota or Sioux people of southwestern Minnesota interpreted the carvings before the arrival of white settlers in large numbers in the nineteenth century. The first known published description of the petroglyphs appeared in a New Ulm newspaper in 1885. In later years, archaeological study of the carvings progressed slowly. Not until 1960 did the petroglyphs receive serious attention, and in 1971 the site underwent an intensive survey and mapping.

The Jeffers carvings give us information about the activities, interests, and spiritual lives of the people who created them. They are also one of the few ways in which American Indians who lived before the eighteenth century can speak directly to us — Indians and non-Indians — without the interference of later historical biases and modern interpreters. Any visitor to the Jeffers Petroglyphs can look and draw his or her own conclusions about the first people to live in the place we call Minnesota.

◄

TRADITIONAL ARTS
Ojibway women working between the late nineteenth and mid-twentieth centuries created the beautiful geometric patterns and floral designs of the beadwork shown here. John Bug, an Ojibway who lived at Mille Lacs for many years, carved the pipestem from a single piece of wood. The balls of nettle twine were made by Maude Kegg — also known as O-mah-dwe — a respected Ojibway storyteller as well as a craftsmaker. Some of these items were collected by Harry and Jeannette Ayer, who operated a trading post at Mille Lacs Lake between about 1918 and the late 1950s.

PETROGLYPHS
This detail of the carvings at the Jeffers site was photographed in 1990 by Jet Lowe, who documented important historic places in Minnesota as part of a nationwide federal survey.

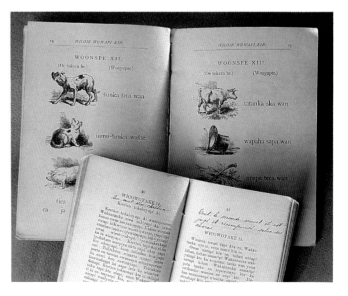

RESERVATION MAP
George A. Ralph, who worked as a U.S. government surveyor on the Red Lake Indian Reservation in northern Minnesota, prepared a map to aid settlers who wished to acquire land when parts of the reservation were opened to settlement in 1896. The Red Lake Nation retained sovereignty on the lands that remained.

Students at reservation schools often learned skills that did not closely match the needs or aesthetics of their own culture. The lace handkerchief on the map was the handiwork of a student at Leech Lake School in 1898.

RED SCHOOL HOUSE
Students at the Red School House in St. Paul, a school for Indian youth, took part in an annual maple sugaring event in Maple Plain in 1980.

DAKOTA BOOKS
The picture dictionary, *Wicoie Wowapi Kin* (The Word Book), was written by the Reverend Alfred Longley Riggs in 1877. An earlier missionary, Father Augustin Ravoux, wrote and published *Wakantanka Ti Ki Chanku* (The Path to the House of God) in 1844 — making him Minnesota's first known printer. This copy belonged to Father Jean Genin, who wrote French translations in the margins.

PORCELAIN DISH
Martye Allen, a contemporary ceramic artist from Minneapolis, echoed the images of the petroglyphs on this porcelain dish crafted in 1987.

ARTIFACTS
Archaeologists recovered these objects of Indian origin dating back as far as 9,000 years ago. The large pot, which was reassembled from many small fragments, was used sometime between 400 and 1,100 years ago. The other items include tools made from a variety of materials: a polished granite celt or axhead, stone or metal arrowheads and spearheads, a hoe made from a bison scapula, and small bone awls.

◄

THE TOMAHAWK
Gus H. Beaulieu was a publishing veteran in 1903 when he founded *The Tomahawk*, a newspaper that originated from the White Earth Reservation. He and a relative, Theodore H. Beaulieu, had earlier published *The Progress*, Minnesota's first reservation paper. In the pages of both publications, Beaulieu frequently criticized the U.S. Office of Indian Affairs for its seemingly arbitrary decisions; he also lambasted tribal leaders for resisting assimilation into white culture.

The photo (above) shows the *Tomahawk* pressroom, about 1910. It was taken by Robert G. Beaulieu — Gus's brother — who was a skilled photographer in the White Earth area.

SNANA AND MARY
Harry Shepherd, a prominent black photographer, took this portrait of Snana and Mary in his St. Paul studio.

WOMAN AND BLUEBERRIES
A 1971 painting by Ojibway artist Patrick Des Jarlait

INDIAN MOTHER, WHITE DAUGHTER

The U.S.–Dakota Conflict of 1862, in southern Minnesota, surely ranks among the bloodiest episodes in the government's mishandling and misunderstanding of Indian affairs. The Dakota had learned that signing treaties with white Americans gave them little protection from land-grabbers and dishonest agents. By 1862 they were reduced to living on a strip of land only ten miles wide that ran along the south side of the Minnesota River. Food supplies promised by the government arrived late, in short quantity, or of inedible quality. Traders charged outrageously high prices for supplies. Furthermore, many Dakota feared that the government's policy of integrating Indians into white society and its customs — such as by training Dakota people to become farmers — would cause the destruction of tribal culture and cohesiveness.

During the summer of 1862, as tensions with traders and settlers peaked, many of the Dakota decided to go to war. Hundreds of people were killed in encounters between Indians, settlers, and soldiers throughout the Minnesota River valley.

Mary Schwandt, a fourteen-year-old member of a German family, was taken prisoner by the warring Dakota. Snana, a Dakota woman, "had taken pity on a little white girl when her life was in great danger," Mary later related, and had cared for her. Mary eventually was freed. Of the eight in her family, only she and a younger brother survived. Thirty-two years later Mary Schwandt Schmidt retold her experiences of 1862 to a reporter for the *St. Paul Pioneer Press*. She praised Snana's kindnesses.

Somehow, the published story reached the Nebraska Santee Agency, where Snana (now using the name Maggie Brass) lived. "She read the story," Mary wrote, "and in a week or ten days she was in St. Paul to see me. I thought she had passed away long ago."

The two women kept in touch for the remainder of Snana's life. On September 28, 1900, Snana wrote this letter to Mary:

My Dear adopted daughter,

I recived your letter. was glad to here from you. I want to tell you what I think about comeing to Mendota. I think it is to cold to come now. I will weat till spring. that is if I live that long. . . . [I]f you can I wish you would send me some wild Rice. I am Sham to say that but I am sick and not feld good. . . . I think about you just as my one child. I never ben home sick when I was with you. I send my best wishes to Mr Schmidt and Carl. . . . I feeld like I went to your house and see you all while I was writeing to you.

your mother
Maggie Brass

On the Farm

THE BOOK FARMER

Oliver H. Kelley was a traveler. He left Boston in 1847 and settled two years later on land near the banks of the Mississippi River, two and a half miles south of the current location of Elk River, Minnesota. Fifteen years later he spent time in Washington, D.C., working as a clerk for the U.S. Department of Agriculture and then for the Post Office Department. He toured the South after the Civil War to learn about the agricultural potential that remained in the war-ravaged states. By 1868 he was back in Minnesota, where he spent several more years and then made more moves before packing his bags for Florida.

Kelley traveled not for adventure, but because he had a lifelong interest in the profession of farming. During his years on his farm near Elk River, he worked hard to develop scientific methods that would bring greater chances of success and greater financial rewards. He experimented with improved breeds of farm animals, new cash crops, the use of better agricultural machinery, and the properties of different types of soil and plants.

Many other Minnesota farmers in the mid-nineteenth century were simply struggling to survive. Although some had received their land free or at low cost from the U.S. government, they had to build their own homes and use oxen and such tools as axes, shovels, and plows to clear their fields and put them into agricultural production. Most farmers grew wheat, corn, or oats. But even when the prices they received for their crops fell, their overhead costs for shipping grain via rail, paying interest on loans, and purchasing equipment remained high.

Like their neighbors, Oliver Kelley and his wife Lucy Earle were not immune from hardship. After the young couple endured a rough Minnesota winter with little more than cranberries and wild rice to eat, Lucy died during childbirth in 1851. Just six months later the baby, who had been named for her mother, also perished.

Although Kelley believed that farming was a noble profession, he saw little nobility in the struggles of Minnesota's farmers. As early as 1852 he helped organize a countywide society of farmers

COMMON WEEDS

In the 1930s the Minnesota Department of Agriculture issued sheets depicting common weeds to help farmers and landowners identify them.

PLAT MAPS

County plat maps from 1888 (top) and 1980 show a century of change in the area that includes the Kelley Farm.

that encouraged them to pool their knowledge and to benefit from each other's experiences. He concluded, though, that more action – much more – was needed to bring farmers closer to gaining financial security from their labors.

So in 1867, while at work in Washington, Kelley founded a new, national agricultural society: the Patrons of Husbandry. He envisioned it as an organization that would use a fraternal structure to bring farmers together as a class to work for their common financial interests. It would be a secret society – similar in its rituals to the Masonic Lodge – that would also emphasize education and promote social and cultural advancement.

The idea generated little interest out East. The following year Kelley returned to Minnesota, where it is likely that his second wife – Temperance Lane Kelley – had followed the example of many farm women by assuming an active role in the management of the land. She and their two daughters had stayed in Minnesota and operated the farm with hired help during Oliver's time in Washington.

Kelley began organizing local chapters of his society, which became popularly known as the Grange. Eventually Grange chapters sprouted all over the state – indeed, all over the midsection of America. Many Minnesota Grangers worked to increase their financial leverage by banding together to sell their harvests and to purchase their supplies and equipment. Some members shared Kelley's enthusiasm for education and cultural progress. Others directed their chapters more directly toward political action, and they succeeded in pushing through the Minnesota legislature several laws regulating the railroad companies. Politics, however, became a divisive issue in the Grange, and few chapters survived beyond the 1880s. The Grange remains active today as an advocacy group for farmers.

The Kelley Farm, a site operated by the Minnesota Historical Society, is a working enterprise that makes use of historical agricultural equipment, old farming methods, and a treasury of heirloom crops that have long vanished from other Minnesota farms. Improved King Philip corn, renowned in the 1850s and 1860s as a particularly productive and fast-growing variety, still waves its tassels on the Kelley Farm, sharing the fields with such crops as Black Norway oats, Early Short Horn carrots, and Maine Yellow Eye beans. Berkshire hogs, Dominique chickens, and other nineteenth-century breeds of farm animals occupy the pens and yards.

Today's animals are different, as are the farmers. Yet Oliver Kelley's dream about improving farm life is reflected in changes that have taken place among farm families far beyond the region of Elk River.

MINNESOTA HARVEST FIELD
In 1877 Joseph R. Meeker painted this scene from a farm on the shores of the Mississippi River at Lake Pepin.

THRESHING MACHINE
A farmer near Marine on St. Croix put this threshing machine to use during the 1860s. It is now used at the Kelley Farm in Sherburne County.

CREAM SEPARATOR

Gordon Wolf used this cream separator on his farm near Princeton in the
1940s.

BUTTER CARTON DRESS

Mary Ann Titrud, crowned Princess Kay of the Milky Way at the 1965 Minnesota State Fair, proudly wore this striking (although uncomfortable) dress constructed from butter cartons.

◄

SEED COMPANY

The historical collections of the Northrup King Company, a premier grower and retailer of seeds for farm and garden, are as colorful as the products themselves. The firm has been especially successful in developing seeds that are adapted for the cold northern climate. In 1895 William King bought five hundred shares of Northrup, Braslan, Goodwin and Company, leading a year later to the formation of Northrup King. The certificate for those shares is one of many items shown here that document the company's management and labor history — ranging from nineteenth-century catalogs and price lists to company newsletters, advertisements, sales samples, merchandising and promotional material, trade signs, feed sacks, packaging and testing equipment, seed kits, and correspondence tied to the old television show, "Queen for a Day." Seed packets carried their own form of advertising: pictures of perfect vegetables and flowers that inspired gardeners to try harder every year.

SEED ADVERTISEMENTS

Northrup King ads from the 1930s were aimed at both farmers and home gardeners.

WINNOWING BASKET

Ojibway wild ricers at Grand Portage used this basket and these ricing sticks in the years before 1930. The continuing vitality of the ricing tradition is reflected in the package of hand-harvested wild rice produced by the Ikwe Marketing Collective of White Earth Reservation.

WILD RICING

Photographers Frances Densmore and Monroe Killy produced many images of the wild rice harvest. Densmore's photo (above) dates from around 1910, Killy's from 1939.

GATHERING PLACE

Tom Arndt, a leading documentary art photographer, portrayed the lives of farm families during the farm crisis of the 1980s. This picture was taken at an auction barn in Sleepy Eye in 1985.

PATCHWORK

Anna Sauglow, a schoolteacher, began hand-patching work clothes for herself and her brother, Selmer, a farmer near Vining, Otter Tail County, in the early 1960s. She added fabric scraps salvaged from pillowcases, bedspreads, and other sources, eventually covering the surfaces of these overalls and skirt with patchwork.

Since the 1880s this same practicality has been reflected in the pages of *The Farmer*, the state's oldest and most influential farming magazine.

STAYING ON THE LAND

"Century farm" is the term for farms that have been in the same family for a hundred years or longer. In 1976 the Minnesota State Fair and *The Farmer* magazine launched a process enabling Minnesota families to receive official century-farm status for their long-held family lands.

One of the many century farm applications came from Ruby Ney and Donald Ney of Henderson. They were, respectively, the grandchild and great-grandchild of Wilhelm and Sophia Gentz Ney, German immigrants who homesteaded the family farm in Le Sueur County beginning in 1859.

Here is an excerpt from the Ney application. It begins after relating how Wilhelm and Sophia immigrated to the United States in the 1850s.

They arrived in St. Paul and being a wood craftsman he was soon involved in his work. Not satisfied with their location and [hearing] stories of land to be had for homesteads up the river they decided to leave. . . .

They arrived in East Henderson by boat on the Minn[esota] river and staked a claim in Hillsdale Township, Le Sueur Co. Hillsdale Twp was re-named to Tyrone Twp by Irish residents after Tyrone County, Ireland in 1858 when Minn became a state.

After clearing an area overlooking the Minn river valley he built a story and a half log house where his sons . . . and daughter . . . were born. The building is still in use. Jan. 1, 1859 he received pre-emption certificate No. 2-229 signed by President Buchanan for the property. It passed on to Henry Ney 1884, Gilbert Ney 1945 and is now operated by great grandson Donald Ney, 1971.

In 1990 the family donated the farm to Le Sueur County for future use as a wildlife game refuge.

BOG SHOES

The familiar crescent-shaped shoes forged by blacksmiths were not the only hoof gear for horses. Strapped onto draft animals that worked low and swampy land, bog shoes kept the horses from becoming stuck in the mire. This pair was made by Andrew O. Palm of Isanti County.

RUST BUSTERS

The National Rust Busters Club was at work in the 1920s controlling the spread of black stem rust – a disease damaging to wheat and other crops. Schoolchildren joined in the fight to eradicate the common barberry bush, which harbored the disease.

FARM MACHINERY

For most of this century, inmates at the Minnesota Correctional Facility in Stillwater have manufactured the "Minnesota" line of farm machinery. In addition to the binder pictured on the left of these catalog covers from the mid-1910s, prisoners also produced cream separators, harvesters, twine, tongue trucks, cultivators, and many other varieties of equipment.

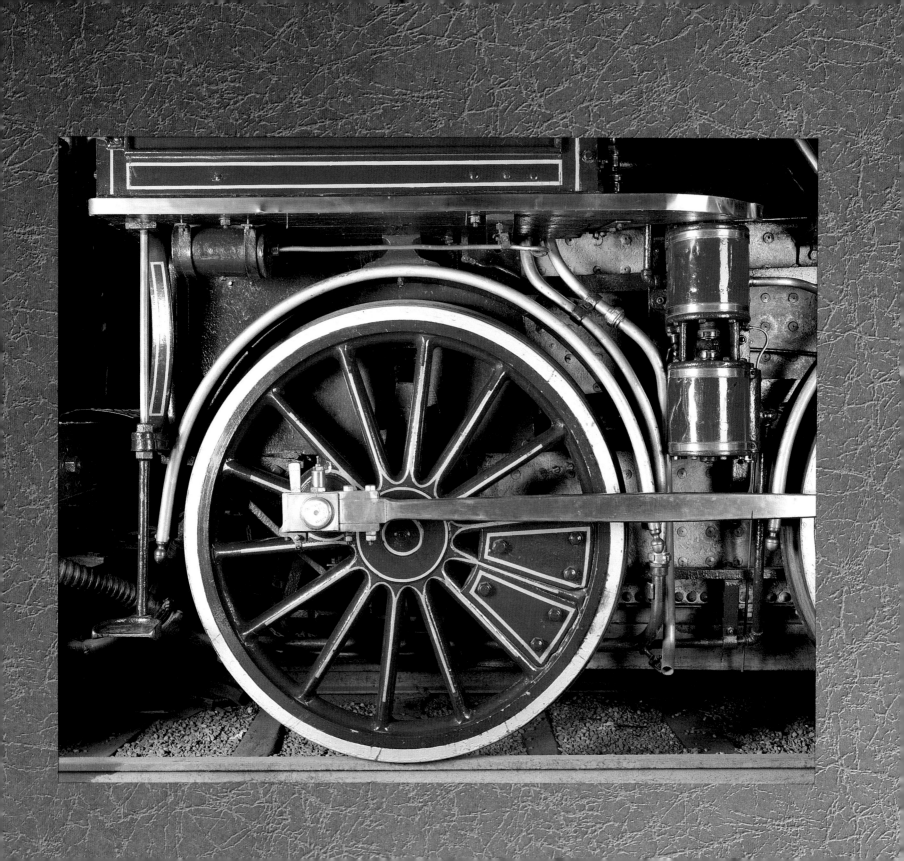

Getting from Here to There

THE DEVIL ON WHEELS

A man named William R. Crooks, born in New York City and schooled at West Point, arrived in St. Paul in 1857 as the first chief engineer of the St. Paul and Pacific Railroad Company. He served in the Sixth Minnesota Infantry Regiment during the U.S.–Dakota Conflict in 1862, spent three years in the Minnesota Legislature, and died in Portland, Oregon, in 1907.

A railroad engine named "William Crooks," built in Paterson, New Jersey, arrived in St. Paul aboard a Mississippi River barge in 1861. A year later, on June 28, 1862, it chugged along a new line of rail stretching about ten miles from St. Paul to St. Anthony — the first passenger railroad run in Minnesota history. The engine survived a serious fire in 1868, endured years of mothballing, and is still with us.

Alas, the human William Crooks, despite his vast knowledge of railroads and his years of public service in the legislature, is but a footnote in Minnesota history compared with the machine that bears his name. The "William Crooks" represents the state's entry into the Industrial Age, an era in which "horsepower" and "footpower" gradually became quaint and old-fashioned notions. Transportation, in particular, changed forever.

Within twenty-five years a web of rails entwined the state, employing thousands, carrying lumberjacks and miners to previously inaccessible areas, giving birth to towns, providing new markets for farmers and manufacturers, and filling the air with whistling screeches, steamy mechanical belches, and clouds of smoke.

At the turn of the century every one of Minnesota's major industries depended on the ever more powerful and numerous descendants of the "William Crooks." Without trains, farmers could only grow food for themselves and their immediate neighbors. Without rails, loggers could only rely on the winter-locked Mississippi and other rivers to move their timber. And without tracks, all the ore in the Iron Range could go nowhere. Not surprisingly, the most influential man in the state was James J. Hill of St. Paul, whose rail empire encompassed virtually the entire Northwest.

And could William Crooks (the man) have imagined that by 1920 the Twin Cities would rank among the nation's top ten railroad centers, with thick corridors of track connecting Minneapolis and St. Paul and then running eastward to the Middle Atlantic seaboard and westward to the Pacific Coast?

By the arrival of the Great Depression the size of Minnesota's rail system had peaked. Autos and trucks had cut into the passenger-moving and goods-hauling business. After a couple more decades, airplanes would steal most of the long-distance travel market.

But the "William Crooks," which started it all, still stands.

"WILLIAM CROOKS"
The famous locomotive was photographed about 1864, soon after its arrival in the state; a detail of one of the wheels is shown on page 42. The "William Crooks" has been on display at the Lake Superior Museum of Transportation in Duluth since 1975.

STEREOGRAPHS

The photographer William Illingworth traveled on railroads and boats to Minnesota places that armchair travelers from other states might want to see. He created and published stereographs, or double-image photos that become three-dimensional when placed in a stereoscope.

SILVER PUNCH BOWL

Upset that Minneapolitans had feted James J. Hill with a celebration to acknowledge the railroad baron's contributions to that city, St. Paul residents presented Hill with this silver punch bowl in 1893. The formal occasion for the gift was Hill's completion of a Great Northern Railway route to the West Coast. Two portraits of Hill, representations of his earliest businesses in St. Paul, a map of the Great Northern rail network, and inscriptions adorn the silver surface.

AIRLINE COMPANIES

The airlines have grown and merged in ways that might best be traced by a family history chart. When Northwest Airlines acquired Republic in 1986, it also inherited materials from a host of predecessor airlines. The Society's collection of documents, flight bags, flight attendant uniforms, food service materials, menus, tickets, and memorabilia for these airlines reaches back to the beginnings of commercial aviation in the 1910s.

AMELIA EARHART

The aviator's 1933 letter to her friend Croil Hunter, who headed Northwest Airlines for thirty-five years, shows the depth of her technical expertise.

SPEED HOLMAN

George "Speed" Holman (left) – Minnesota's second most famous flyer, after Charles A. Lindbergh, Jr. – flew this plane to a $10,000 first prize in a 1927 National Air Derby from New York to Spokane. Heading home, Holman lost engine power while flying over the Montana mountains at five hundred feet and glided for fifteen miles among the peaks before landing without mishap. Holman was killed at air races in Omaha in 1931.

AMELIA EARHART

Locust Avenue,
Rye, New York

March 9, 1933.

Dear Croil:

I am glad Robert Gross is calling on you Monday. I think you will like to do business with him and his gang.

Concerning specifications for the twin-engined Lockheed, Paul Collins expressed himself as satisfied with details of construction, motors, gear, sound-proofing, instruments and their arrangement, as well as with all "gadgets". Thus the requirements to insist on boil down to important ones of capacity and load distribution, speed, power plant specifications, and radio equipment.

Under the first it seems advisable to have 10 passenger seats, 2 pilot places, 4 gasoline tanks holding 40 gals. each, and a 300 pound baggage compartment. This arrangement could be used in any combination of passengers, pilots, mail and gasoline, depending on the run.

As to speed, the planes should cruise 180 MPH at 85% motor output. With flaps, the landing speed should not be more than 65 MPH, though a higher one would not be a valid cause for much concern, in my opinion. Take-off and climb are not very important in commercial flying.

Two motors are only a nuisance unless altitude with full pay load can be maintained at 4000 ft. by means of one engine alone.

In considering radio equipment I believe serious thought should be given to the necessity of two-way transmission. It is of course desirable in some instances but before you plan to sacrifice other features to make sending possible I should advise a thorough check in the light of high speed operation. It may be that reception

---

AMELIA EARHART

-2-

of the beam and weather reports will be found all that is essential. I shall talk with you more about this later. As with radio, please think in terms of high speed operation when you juggle the variables of load, gasoline capacity and pay load, as enumerated in the first paragraph.

For instance, remember that with shorter runs the necessity for two pilots diminishes.

Paul Collins suggested to Lockheed officials that they were wasting space by having the cabin as wide as it is. He said it could be decreased by 6", which reduction would tend to increase speed and facilitate flying on one motor, because the power plants could be brought in closer to the cabin. Further, such reduction would not interfere with passenger comfort.

You will find that in ordering ships on paper the purchaser will probably be required to put up 20% of the final price. This amount cares for the engines, which manufacturers will not supply on credit. Ownership of the engines would be your protection should the deal fall through because specifications were not lived up to.

If the foregoing does not cover what you want, telegraph me at Rye.

Sincerely yours,

Croil Hunter, Esq.,
Northwestern Airways,
St.Paul, Minn.

P.S. While talking with Gross you might sound him out on the possibility of gearing the motors. Pratt & Whitney have told me gearing would add about 250 lbs. in weight. However, speed and efficiency might be increased to offset this load. I am looking into the details of this further.

BETTER ROADS

The Bjorlees, whose travel album is at left in this picture, told of their adventures on Minnesota's back roads. Over the years the people who lived along those roads petitioned officials to improve them. These 1885 petitions to the board of supervisors of Silver Creek Township, Wright County, urged better roads and cartways.

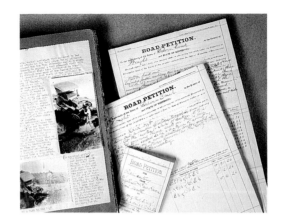

THE ROAD HARDLY TRAVELED

An auto journey from New York to Lake of the Woods: Today's drivers might look forward to such a trip as pleasant and serene — not as thrilling, unpredictable, and dangerous.

But in 1916, when Ignatius and Cornelia Bjorlee set out upon their east-to-west journey in their Model T Ford, cross-country motoring required patience, luck, and a strong constitution. Gas stations were far-flung and roads sometimes barely discernible. The driver's main concerns were not air-conditioning failures but plunges into swamps, impassable stretches of muck, and the frequent absence of road signs of any kind.

En route to a lake cabin that Ignatius's family owned at Lake of the Woods, the Bjorlees carefully recorded their adventures. Later they typed their notes in a scrapbook with photos. Here is Ignatius's account of a not-too-unusual day as they neared their destination:

> We encountered a long narrow stretch of very treacherous sand, not far from Perham, and taking advantage of my lack of experience with such road beds, the Flivver suddenly plunged headlong into the marsh. Cornelia amused herself by watching the tadpoles, as they swam around our radiator hood, while I toiled wearily along the sandy road for a distance of more than two miles, in search of some good natured farmer who would render his aid. No body home. Had to wait until the family returned from church before my wants could be made known.

> To us the name [Ogema] recalls swamp, for it was near this town that later in the day we arrived at a point where all traces of a road vanished, and we found it optional with us to select one out of a dozen or more trails. It was evident that motorists did not travel over this rout[e], but we had no alternative. By stepping from one bog to another Cornelia walked across, on what appeared to her to be the best path, and placed sticks in the tall grass for my guidance. I scarcely know how it was managed, but the Ford literally sailed through.

BJELLA AUTOMOBILE

It could cruise along at twenty miles per hour. It had a two-cylinder, air-cooled engine. It was manufactured in McIntosh, Minnesota.

The Bjella automobile, the creation of a Norwegian-born blacksmith, never attained mass production. In fact, Ole Bjella made only one car, during the winter of 1905–06. Although there were 2,500 registered autos in the state in 1905, this was the first that anyone in the Polk County town of McIntosh had ever owned – much less built. Bjella was unable to get the financing he needed to produce more. So he returned to blacksmithing and making sleighs and harrows. He died in 1940.

HIGHWAY MAPS

Traveling the highways before 1920 was a mess – there was little consistency in the names given to roads from one county to another. Charles M. Babcock of Elk River, who became a member of the state highway commission in 1913 and later served as the commissioner of highways, lamented this sorry state of affairs. In the 1920s he developed a uniform system of numbering highways and worked to pass a constitutional amendment that financed the building of good roads in the state.

Of course, a good seat cushion, like this one dating from between 1900 and 1920, could accomplish almost as much as a good map in making an auto journey pleasant in the days before shock absorbers.

HIGH BRIDGE

Torn down and replaced in the 1980s, the old High Bridge in St. Paul did more than carry traffic across the Mississippi River. It also inspired poets and gave artists a distinctive subject. Gaylord Schanilec created this 1987 wood engraving showing the demolition of the bridge.

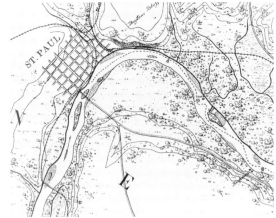

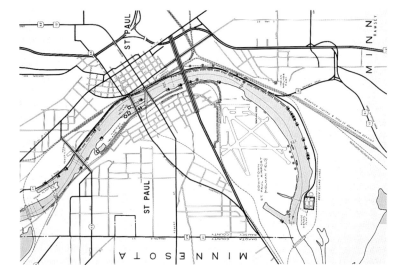

RIVER NAVIGATION

The U.S. Army Corps of Engineers has long produced navigation charts for the Mississippi River. One done in 1878 (above) shows the location of roads, railroads, the steamboat channel, dams, bridges, and even riverboat wrecks. The later map dates from 1975.

BICYCLE LAMP
A battery-powered bicycle lamp from the early twentieth century

SNOWMOBILE
Minnesotans have driven snowmobiles to the North Pole, and there is no shortage of them in the state's recreational areas. This model, manufactured by Polaris of Roseau, bears the stenciled message, "We go in snow."

Labor Days

WORKING THE FORESTS

They did more than saw down trees. They cooked potatoes and flapjacks, branded logs, built camps, put together rafts of logs to float downriver, mapped tracts of timber, dynamited logjams in the rivers, and lorded it over one another. Starting in the 1840s the forests of Minnesota swarmed with lumberjacks. In the early years most of the state's logging workers were men born in America, French Canadians, Scots, or Englishmen. After 1870 Scandinavians joined their ranks, and Finnish immigrants brought their skills to the forests beginning in the 1890s. At the dawn of the twentieth century Minnesota claimed forty thousand lumberjacks.

Minnesota's lumberjacks worked hard and effectively: so effectively, in fact, that by 1910 most of the state's great white and red pine stands had been cleared. During the peak logging year of 1900, these workers harvested a billion board feet of lumber.

For much of that busy era lumberjacks came to work armed only with saws, axes, and other hand tools. They loaded the cut logs onto sleighs that oxen or horses pulled to the river or railhead where the logs were transported to sawmills. For that labor the men typically earned $1.50 per day and received food and housing in the logging company's camp.

The turn-of-the-century bunkhouses of the lumberjacks were no model of comfort and tidiness. Up to eighty men slept in a single building, with smoke from wood-burning stoves often filling the air. Dirty and wet clothing hung from wires stretched across the room. The men slept on straw mattresses laid on bunks that were built along the walls, with one blanket to cover the mattress and another to put on top.

With such harsh living and working conditions — and with liquor often banned in the camps — many lumberjacks understandably felt inclined to cut loose during their infrequent trips into nearby towns. There they sought booze and prostitutes.

Like the herding of cattle in the Wild West, logging lent itself to romanticizing and myth-making. Lumberjacks commonly told tall tales during their time off in the bunkhouse. Until the

Red River Lumber Company printed some Paul Bunyan stories in 1914, however, it is doubtful that the workers knew many of those instant legends about Paul, Babe the Blue Ox, and the other characters who became famous across America.

Despite the tales, few loggers found romance in their work. Instead, they faced exploitation from their employers. In 1916 loggers tried to organize, demanding higher wages, shorter workdays, better lodging and food, and the freedom to form unions without harassment. A thousand lumberjacks walked off their jobs and out of the woods in January 1917. Working with the lumber companies, officials in towns like Virginia broke the strike by banning the distribution of union literature, arresting leaders of the walkout, and spreading stories of terroristic acts by the strikers.

By then, however, the logging industry was declining as the supply of pine timber was depleted. Sawmills throughout the state began closing as early as 1910, and by the 1930s only a handful were left.

Logging remains an occupation in Minnesota to this day. More than three thousand workers were employed in harvesting second-growth trees during the 1980s, although in a form much changed from the days of handsaws and axes. Nowadays lumber workers cut, gather, and move timber using new tools of the trade: tractor-mounted feller bunchers, mechanized skidders, and whole-tree chippers.

That is progress, and many other Minnesota occupations have made similar gains over the decades. But there is still a gulf between work and play, and maybe it will always be that way.

◄

BOAT MAKER
Starting in the late nineteenth century, the shop of J. G. Schmidt in St. Paul was busy turning out motor launches and other boat-related equipment. Here is a sampling of the manufacturer's shop equipment, tools, and supplies. The shop closed in 1935.

PAUL BUNYAN
The tall tales of Paul Bunyan, Babe the Blue Ox, and other characters began receiving wide circulation in 1914 when the Red River Lumber Company adapted stories of the legendary crew as part of an advertising promotion. Within ten years Bunyan had become a national institution.

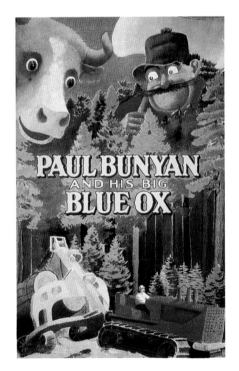

LUMBERJACKS

Itinerant photographer William T. Roleff visited northern Minnesota lumber camps and sawmills from 1912 to 1918, taking pictures that the men bought to show to family and friends. Roleff later opened a studio in Two Harbors and became a staff photographer for the *Duluth News Tribune*.

TIMBERHOG

This two-person chain saw was used by forestry workers in the 1940s.

◄

UNDERWEAR

Northwestern Knitting's union suit, a combination undergarment made of silk-plated wool, brought such comfort to the consumer of the 1890s that George D. Munsing's place in the underwear market was secured. His Minneapolis firm, which later became Munsingwear, began more than a century of innovation in the knitwear business. Brightly printed Vassarette lingerie and Grand Slam golf shirts were introduced in the 1950s. In addi-tion to corporate records, the Minnesota Historical Society holds about three thousand examples of garments, product packing, and marketing merchandise from the early 1880s to the 1980s.

INSIDE THE MILL

In 1921, when this picture was taken inside Munsingwear's eight-story Minneapolis plant, the firm was the largest employer of women in the state.

Yarn Winding Department

THE LIFE OF A SEAMSTRESS

Abbie T. Griffin, a nineteenth-century Minneapolis seamstress, described her daily routine in her journal, which noted events of the years 1882–85:

> Friday, September 1st [1882]
> Warm. Have been so rushed all day and tonight am so tired. This is mother's birthday, she is sixty four years old. I am so sorry not to be able to give her a treat.
>
> Saturday, [September] 2nd
> Hot. Was so hurried to get the skirt done but I finished it & went down after dinner, brought home a stripe for an afgahn [sic], peacock blue felt to be embroidered with wild roses. Commenced.
>
> Monday, [September] 4th
> Lovely. Got up early and as mother is not at all well I had all the work to do and then the washing but it was all done by noon. Worked on the stripe after dinner. . . .
>
> Tuesday, October 16th, 1883
> It is nearly a year since I have written in my journal and so much has happened of interest to me. I will note a few of them.
>   The last of November I poisoned my eyes with the stamping liquid and for the rest of the winter could not see

to read or write or sew. Mother was so sick all winter too and has had such a hard summer. . . .
      This day I am thirty two years old and a quiet day it has been. This morning I did up my work. . . . Went over to Nellie's & she cut me a velvet vest for my black broadcloth jacket.

UNIFORM

A maid's uniform and garment pattern from about 1915

OSCAR HOWARD
The entrepreneur (left) with a display of his firm's wares

FROM '36 CHEVROLET TO 32,000 MEALS IN A WEEK

Entrepreneurs usually have a strong drive for independence. Oscar C. Howard, who moved to the Twin Cities from Alabama in 1950, fiercely wanted a business of his own. After working six years in the food service department of Twin City Arsenal, he resolved to become a caterer. An experienced bookkeeper told him he could not possibly start a business on only three hundred dollars. Howard decided to try anyway, and in 1986 he recounted his rise to success as a business owner:

> I started out running my business out of the back end of a '36 Chevrolet. Eventually I moved into a 20' by 10' office. In the early '60s, I bought a building for my company. I started out with one client—the Bell Telephone Company—serving coffee breaks for their safety meetings. Eventually, I was catering the Company picnics. . . .
>
> . . . I worked hard. I worked long hours. And I never lost sight of my goal, even when I was discouraged, even when I went to the bank for a loan and they asked to see my balance sheet. I told them I had no balance or a sheet. When they wouldn't give me a loan, I refused to quit. . . .

In the late 1960s, I was asked by the president of the Office of Equal Opportunity if I would consider taking over a feeding program for the government in Minneapolis. . . . I took this project because I saw a need to be fulfilled. In one year's time, my staff and I built this program up so we were eventually serving 32,000 meals a week.

My staff and I later started the Meals On Wheels program for the elderly in Minneapolis. . . . This concept is being used all over the state of Minnesota. . . .

. . . I am now developing and marketing new food products under the name of Howard's Frozen Foods, Inc. All of this came out of a company which could not get credit for one turkey.

RED RUDENSKY
The former lockpick posing with a display of door locks

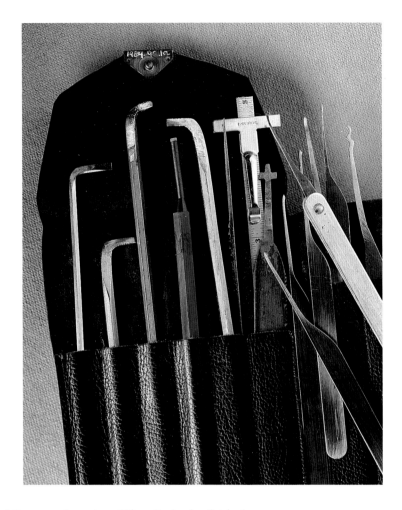

LOCK-PICKING TOOLS

Red Rudensky's working tools were a bit unorthodox.

Today we might call Rudensky a midlife career changer. What they called him several decades ago was a reformed crook. Rudensky, born in 1899, had gone into petty crime as a child in New York City. He spent time in reform school, moved to the Midwest, worked for Al Capone and Bugs Moran, and masterminded a series of heists in Illinois and Missouri.

Based on skills he learned in Minneapolis, he gained a reputation as one of the country's most skilled safecrackers and lockpicks. But the law caught up with Rudensky, and he spent more than twenty-five years behind bars – twice escaping from Leavenworth Prison in Kansas.

While in prison Rudensky met Charles A. Ward, later president of the St. Paul firm of Brown & Bigelow, who was serving time on a drug charge. Ward urged Rudensky to aban-

don crime. When Rudensky finished his sentence, he accepted Ward's offer to work for him as a copywriter, specializing in writing material for the publishing firm's religious calendars.

In the 1960s Rudensky made the ultimate turnaround. He worked as a consultant for 3M's home security business, where his criminal background provided a highly valued perspective.

OFFICE WORK
Women office workers, photographed by the Norton & Peel studio in 1938 (top) and 1949

GIVING SECRETARIES THEIR DUE
In about 1970 political activist and feminist Arvonne Fraser prepared a speech to deliver during National Secretaries Week. Here are the rough notes she jotted down in advance:

It's natl secys wk
florists urged bouquets

I'd recommend a raise for most sec'ys are over-worked and underpaid – and a good new sec'y is hard to find – if you are trying to hire one. Someone has said there's no such thing as a secretary because if she's good she's an executive and if she's not so hot she's a clerk-typist.

But I'm concerned these days with the *undervaluing* the denigration of secretaries & their work – with women & their work – and tho' I'm active in the women's movement I'm ashamed to admit – that it is women *undervaluing* their own work [and] their sister's work that concerns me. . . .

Stand up for yourselves – your rights – and for your sisters –

Realize & exercise your own power – world can't get along w/o you.

TRAMP REGISTRY

Many cities and towns have grappled with the measures they should take to house – or, in some cases, keep out – unemployed people wandering the state. Brainerd kept a registry of tramps who were given overnight lodging in the city jail. Most had no money or possessions other than the clothing they wore. This page shows entries from 1910.

THE STOCKYARDS

The first stockyard in St. Paul opened in 1886 to attract business from cattle raisers in the region who until then had to ship their animals to Chicago for slaughter. With thirty-six companies in operation, employment in the St. Paul stockyards peaked just after World War II. Then came a slow decline, with closings and layoffs. In recent years only a handful of companies and their employees have remained. This insurance map dates from 1939. The sticking knife did its work at Armour Meat's South St. Paul stockyard, in operation between 1919 and 1979.

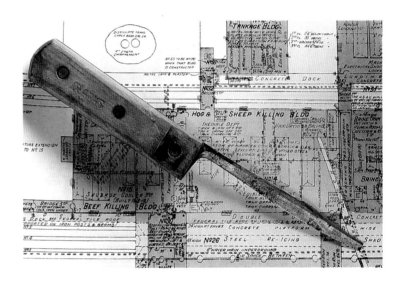

STRIKEBREAKER'S CLUB

In the 1920s the Twin City Rapid Transit Company distributed strikebreakers' clubs to supervisors during times of labor turmoil in Minneapolis. Objects like this are part of labor history, which is also preserved in documents and photographs that record the growth and activities of individual unions and labor leaders.

A Wealth of Cultures

Den norske Amerikalinje A/S.

NEW WORLD SYMPHONY

When the Bohemian composer Antonín Dvořák briefly sojourned in the Twin Cities in 1893, he had already written his famous *New World* Symphony and was one of the world's most renowned musicians. In St. Paul he endured a somewhat embarrassingly grand welcome by members of the growing Czech community. He also spent time in Minneapolis, where he took in the sight of Minnehaha Falls, which he had long anticipated seeing. Dvořák evidently did not visit the muddy, ramshackle, and vibrant vision of the Old World that sprawled in the shadow of the Washington Avenue Bridge and was called Bohemian Flats.

Not only Bohemians lived in this oft-flooded settlement hugging the west bank of the Mississippi, within sight of the square brick buildings of the University of Minnesota across the river. Immigrants from Slovakia, Ireland, Sweden, Denmark, and Poland also called it home during the neighborhood's existence from around 1870 to the 1930s. Although its houses lacked running water, sewage hookups, and easy access to the rest of the city — one had to climb long, rickety wooden stairways to mount the river bluffs — the settlement was fiercely defended by its residents when the city issued eviction orders in the 1920s to clear the land on behalf of absentee landowners.

There were no Bohemian Flats landowners, tenants, or squatters through the 1860s. Until then the area had a reputation as an especially scenic section of the riverbank that sprouted with butternut and hickory trees. First came a Danish family, followed by a few Bohemians, Slovaks, Germans, and Poles. A group of several dozen Gaelic-speaking immigrants from the Connemara district in Ireland built homes there. Still well outside the places of main settlement in Minneapolis, the land was open and cheap to rent. By 1887 the area had grown into a recognizable neighborhood, with two distinct tiers: an upper flat and a lower flat. Because there were no streets, the wooden houses — often hammered together from boards and other scraps that drifted downriver from the sawmills — faced all directions.

Gradually three main arteries took shape: high-rent Mill Street, moderately priced Cooper Street, and Wood Street – closest to the river and cheapest. Residents along all three streets grew garlic, celery, and parsley in gardens of rich soil dredged up from the river bottom, and some flats dwellers raised rabbits and chickens. Everybody worked. Men took jobs in flour mills, lumber mills, and coopering shops, women labored in the houses and gardens, older girls found work in a nearby pickle factory, and even elderly people and young children made money by harvesting the logs and scrap wood that floated down the river.

Frequently, during spring floods, the river tried to take hold of the community itself. In many of the lowest-lying households, it was an annual ritual to evacuate furniture to buildings on higher ground while the Mississippi, swollen with melted ice, deposited a layer of sand inside the home. Occasionally entire houses drifted off their foundations.

Over the years Bohemian Flats continued to grow until five hundred people lived there. Pedestrians walking across the Washington Avenue Bridge might hear the sounds of accordion, violin, and bagpipe music drifting up from below; see worshipers headed for the nearby Lutheran, Catholic, or Baptist churches; or catch a whiff of sauerkraut, mushroom soup, or potato dumplings on the stove.

By about 1915 Minneapolis planners were preparing to clear the settlement. At the same time, landowners who claimed to hold title to property in the community wanted to evict residents who were not paying rent. In 1923 police attempting to boot out squatters faced rioting residents who were armed with sticks and broom handles.

The people of Bohemian Flats showed their mettle during that fracas, but the war was already lost. By 1932 the community had dwindled to just a handful of houses as the city bought out landowners and began construction of a new barge landing. A few houses that huddled together far from the barge facility survived into the 1940s, but they looked isolated and threatened – much different from the confident appearance that the bustling, ethnically mixed neighborhood boasted in its heyday.

◄

CHINESE COOKING
Ye Sing Woo, together with two brothers and a cousin, started a laundry in downtown Minneapolis in 1883. By 1905 they were ready to open a restaurant – the Yuen Faung Low, or "Cafe of Many Distant Vistas." It operated at its location on Sixth Street near Nicollet Avenue until 1967. A portion of the restaurant's ornate sign is shown with a wok shovel that the cooks in Duluth's Jade Fountain Restaurant used during the first half of this century.

AMISH QUILT

A quilt made in 1987 by Lena Miller, a professional quilter and member of an Amish community at Preston in Fillmore County. In accord with her religious convictions, she lives — and produces her quilts — without the aid of electricity.

RECORDING THE HERITAGE

Writers record their different heritages: a Jewish neighborhood in St. Paul, the vibrant Bohemian Flats, the homeland experiences of members of a Hmong Boy Scout troop. The Hmong are one of several Asian groups that began settling in Minnesota in large numbers in the 1970s. Most arrived from mountainous regions of Laos, where they had fought the North Vietnamese in a guerrilla army supported by the United States government. By 1990 more than sixteen thousand Hmong lived in the state, most of them in the Twin Cities.

SWEDE HOLLOW

St. Paul's version of Bohemian Flats was Swede Hollow, which sat along Phalen Creek below the Seventh Street Bridge. The isolated neighborhood began as a predominantly Scandinavian gathering of shacks, but Italian, Irish, and Mexican families later moved in. Artist Wilbur Hausener, the son of German immigrants, often painted the houses and people of Swede Hollow. When he made this view in the mid-1930s he called it *Italian Village behind Hamm's Brewery.*

JEWISH CULTURE

Jews and the institutions that they developed in the state have been a part of Minnesota life since territorial days. The colorful cloth in the background was used to cover a bema or synagogue lectern sometime during the late nineteenth and early twentieth centuries. Against it are shown a newsletter from Hadassah, the Jewish women's service organization; an 1898 naturalization document issued for Jacob Firestone; and a 1967 marriage certificate.

WINTER IN THE HOLLOW

A 1910 photograph by Albert Munson

FAMILY HEIRLOOMS

A brooch, stickpin, and cuff links owned by a Minnesota family during the late nineteenth century

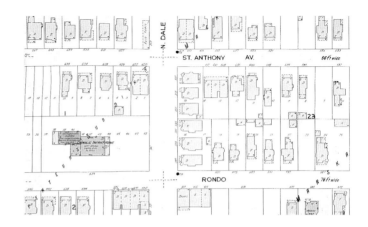

BAPTISMS AND DANCES

Mexican immigrants and other Hispanic people began arriving in Minnesota in sizable numbers in the 1920s. In many of the state's Hispanic communities, the new residents strongly wanted to retain what they could of their family traditions. In 1975 two longtime St. Paul residents participating in an oral history project recalled their families' traditional ways of celebrating special events:

Did your family celebrate baptisms?

My manner of celebrating a baptism is the same as my ancestors'. I would sit four *compadres*. On the decorated table I would put a plate of dessert, the best of whatever I had, and four cups of chocolate. You cross the four cups and everyone drinks from the cup and then they return to the others. This signifies friendship. It shows that whatever you have you are willing to share. What is good for one is also good for the other. You only take one drink of each cup. That is how I do it and my grandmother did it, too.

— Carlotta Arellano

When you arrived [in 1923], did the Mexican people here get together for festivals?

Oh, sure. One of the first organizations that my husband became a member of was the Azteca Club. There were more Mexican people by then, so we used to have dances and parties. We used to celebrate the 24th of December and have festivals at the church. . . . Both the Anahuac and Azteca Clubs would get together and have dances. . . . We used to have a lot of fun. . . . At that time I had only two children. I remember we used to eat at a big table on the corner and if any of the children went to sleep, we would lay them on the table. We did this for many years until finally the custom of taking children to festivities changed. It is not done anymore.

— Petra T. Zepeda

RONDO AVENUE

Long the main artery of St. Paul's black community, Rondo Avenue was wiped off the city map when Interstate Highway 94 was constructed in the 1960s. The neighborhood had been the location of thriving businesses, homes, and churches.

◀

MAURICE CARLTON ARTWORK

"When you want to make something useful, learn to improvise. Put your imagination to work, some will power and self training; you may find your creative capacity."

Maurice Carlton, a retired train attendant with the Northern Pacific Railway, spoke and believed those words. In 1967, a year of high racial tension around the country and in the Twin Cities, he used his imagination and artistic talents to form an unusual alliance with the Inner City Youth League, an organization for black youths in St. Paul. Carlton enlisted the help of young people at the center in making his unique artworks, many from salvaged materials.

GRAVE MARKER
An old Norwegian grave marker from a Minnesota cemetery

IS ASSIMILATION THE RIGHT ROAD?

In September 1946, with World War II barely a year in the past, Japanese Americans faced lingering bigotry and resentment over Japan's role in the war. That month the Japanese American Service Committee of Minneapolis issued a statement of purpose reflecting the group's struggle with the issue of assimilation versus ethnic identity:

> The Japanese-Americans in our community have been accepted cordially and . . . the process of integration is well under way. We feel that they have been received not merely as another racial minority but rather as fellow Americans and therefore they cannot be rightly called "a minority problem." . . .
>
> [W]e of the Service Committee would recommend:
>
> . . . that the J.A.C.L. [Japanese American Citizens' League] focus its attention to the field of political education and legislative action for the Japanese-Americans.
>
> . . . that social activities of the J.A.C.L. be kept at a minimum to avoid undue attention called to Japanese-Americans as a group. Rather, work should be carried on to further acceptance as individual American citizens which comes mainly through personal action. . .
>
> . . . that the possibility of calling the local chapter by some name deleting the term "Japanese American" be considered, such as for example The Urban League which works in behalf of the Negro.

CHANGING NEIGHBORHOODS

Neighborhoods rarely remain static. Especially in larger towns and cities, one ethnic group supplants another as the years pass. These St. Paul City Directory pages show changes in the names of residents between 1929 (left) and 1961 on the West Side along State Street, now the site of an industrial park. More details about community change can be found in the records of the West Side Neighborhood House, one of many settlement houses that have been a part of Twin Cities history.

LAOTIAN EMBROIDERY

Some of Minnesota's Laotian artists have adapted their talents to American applications. This checkbook cover was embroidered by Thu Vang, who lives in St. Paul.

157 Komer Froen Rev ⓪
158 Macarovsky Jerome fish

Texas intersects

159 Bratter Joseph A ⓪
160 Schribman Harry ⓪
161 Mason Wm M
162 Karter Louis ⓪
163 Gerr Pauline Mrs ⓪
    Gerr Max
    Gerr Morris
164 Vacant 1st fl
    Bach Hyman ⓪
    Pleason Nathan
165 Gerr Bros meats
166 Laderman Saml ⓪
167 Kaplan Baruch gro
    Reyer Saml
169 Rosenblom Saml ⓪
170 Goldberg Morris ⓪
172 La Valle David J

Chicago av intersects

174 Neren Aaron ⓪
    Frautschi J J & Sons

157 Monita Alex
Texas begins
159 No return
160 Luna Lazaro G
161 Vacant
162 Avaloz Gabriel G ◎
    △CA4-9788
163 Gerr Morris ◎
    △CA4-3067
    Felipe Santos
164 Berkovitz Esther Mrs ◎
    △CA2-5635
    Vega Jose V
165 Gerr David Kosher
    Meats & Groceries
    △CA4-3067
166 Laderman Pearl Mrs ◎
    △CA4-8802
167 Soto Aristeo
    Vasquez Jose A
    △CA4-4258
169 Rosenblum Myer ◎
    △CA2-7646

State of the Art

MILLIONS OF SKETCHES

About to die in 1908 after a year-long illness, Anton Gág spoke his final words: *"Was der Papa nicht thun konnt, muss die Wanda halt fertig machen."* Translated from German, that last utterance means, "What Papa was unable to accomplish, Wanda will have to finish."

Wanda Gág, then a fifteen-year-old schoolgirl living in New Ulm, realized that her father was not instructing her to care for the family business or to keep the household garden flourishing. Anton was telling her to become an artist.

It was not an unusual expectation, given the background and day-to-day activities of the nine-member Gág family. Anton, a native Czech, was a skilled painter of pictures who had earned a living by running a photography studio and receiving commissions to paint murals and decorate the interiors of public buildings. His wife, Elisabeth Biebl Gág, an Austrian immigrant, assisted in the photo studio before the children were born. The parents encouraged their seven children, of whom Wanda was the eldest, to express themselves creatively. All of the Gág youngsters drew, and several of them — Wanda in particular — studied the art magazines and books of reproductions that filled Anton's attic studio.

To comply with her father's deathbed request and to satisfy her own artistic aspirations, Wanda searched for a way to use her talents to make money for the family. She hit upon the idea of making and selling greeting cards and window displays. She also sent her drawings to magazines and newspapers. In the first two years after her father's death, the *Minneapolis Journal* alone published a ten-part set of fairy tales that Wanda had written and illustrated, four poems, four stories, and thirty-five pictures. It was a hint of the artistic and literary success to come.

But before success came frustration and hardship. With financial assistance from friends, Wanda attended two Twin Cities art schools, the St. Paul School of Art and the Minneapolis School of Art. Her teachers tried to tame her of what they perceived as a wildness in her art; instead of impulsively drawing whatever pleased her, they wanted her to imitate the methods and subjects of the masters. Still, Wanda benefited greatly from her time as a Twin Cities art student, especially by getting to know such fellow students as Adolf Dehn and Harry Gottlieb.

In 1917 Gág won a scholarship to attend classes at the Art Students League in New York City. She moved to the East but took only a year of classes before she had to concentrate on earning an income for her siblings, who had moved from New Ulm to Minneapolis after their mother died. Remaining in New York, Gág labored at a string of commercial art jobs: designing toys, making fashion illustrations, painting lampshades. That meager existence lasted several years before the other Gág children became self-supporting.

By then Gág craved artistic freedom. At the age of thirty she rented an isolated cottage in Connecticut and worked on projects of her own devising—a torrent of artwork that broke free of commercial restraints. In 1926 she exhibited her first one-person show. It brought her national attention, and a reviewer for the *New Yorker* favorably compared her prints and drawings to those of Matisse. It was the start of a rapid upturn in her artistic fortunes. Seeking out another rural setting to use as a studio, she eventually bought a farm near the town of Milford, New Jersey. Seemingly the woman reared in small-town Minnesota worked best far from the commotion of the city.

During the late 1920s Gág moved her work in a new direction. In 1928 she published *Millions of Cats*, a children's book that she wrote as well as illustrated. After years of study and development as an artist, she happily returned to the storybook format that had first brought her recognition as a young contributor to the pages of the *Minneapolis Journal*. Many other children's books followed, including *Snippy and Snappy, Gone Is Gone, Nothing-at-All*, and several books of her own translations of fairy tales of the Grimm brothers.

Minnesota artists need no longer leave the state, as Gág did, to pursue opportunities for their work. She did what she felt she must to follow her father's advice and to remain true to the artistic impulses that were inseparably woven with her spirit. Even so, the upbringing and training that she received in New Ulm and the Twin Cities remained central to her work and character.

◄

ROCK STAR
Prince's motion-picture debut in *Purple Rain*, filmed in Minnesota and released in 1984, established the Minneapolis-based rock star as more than a purely musical talent. The movie tells the story of a singer's ascent from a troubled youth that included poverty and alcoholic parents. This is one of Prince's costumes from *Purple Rain*, shown with a poster from his later film, *Cherry Moon*.

ART COLLECTIVE
Members of WARM—the Women's Art Registry of Minnesota, which was founded in 1975—used their artistic talents to imagine the different directions that the art collective might take in the future. This is one of a remarkable series of drawings that embodied their goals and aspirations.

SELF-PORTRAIT
Wanda Gág drew this pastel self-portrait in 1915, when she was twenty-two and a student at the Minneapolis School of Art.

MILLIONS OF CATS
Wanda Gág's first children's book — *Millions of Cats*, published in 1928 — is also her most popular.

ARTIST'S TOOLS

The easel, palette, and color guides of Cameron Booth, one of many Minnesota artists – including James Rosenquist, LeRoy Neiman, and Paul Manship – who gained a national following. Booth painted *Summer Solstice*, shown on the facing page, in 1954.

NOTHING-AT-ALL

In 1941 Wanda Gág was busy at work on a new project. In a letter to a friend she described what went into the creation of an illustrated children's book:

> How I've worked on that *Nothing-at-all!* I believe I told you I draw it all on glass & its a very lengthy process. For months I've been working 10 to 14 hours a day on it – it is finally all drawn & the plates & proofs made. I think it looks very good. . . . [S]ince this is my first book in color I was pretty nervous about it. . . . You see I draw all three plates in *black*, & its pretty hard to know, for instance, how heavy a drawing will look when its translated into green or red or worse still, how it will look with green superimposed over the red! . . .
>
> On top of everything else we had several bad heatwaves (I'm in N.Y. all the time) *and* I've been fighting some kind of "contact allergy" . . . on my hands. . . .
>
> *Millions of Cats* was done under great physical discomfort too (my left breast was very painful & I was greatly depressed, fearing it might be a tumor) so maybe its a good omen. I mean, maybe it will go well too.

IRON LILY

Not all notable artworks are made by professional artists. An anonymous blacksmith of the 1880s made this sculpture of lilies in a pot.

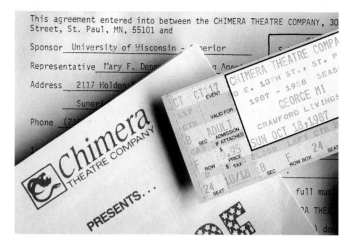

CHIMERA THEATRE

St. Paul's Chimera Theatre mounted hundreds of shows between 1969 and 1987, when it closed down.

HANDICRAFTS

Glazed ceramic teapot and cups, made by Duluth potter Robert Husby in 1988, are shown with a copper jardinière produced by the Handicraft Guild of Minneapolis sometime between 1904 and 1918.

COSTUMES

The beaded and fringed vest in the center was made by Ernie Sam of Mille Lacs Reservation about 1960; it is part of a grass dance costume. Other moods are suggested in the Jack of Diamonds tunic created by Rock in 1981 and the floral print hat made by Jan Shafer in 1990.

THE SOUND OF MUSIC

Born in Minneapolis in 1886, Beatrice Gjertsen Bessesen attended the University of Minnesota and went to Europe where she performed as an opera singer in such works as *Lohengrin*, *Der Rosenkavalier*, and *Tannhäuser*. State heads including Kaiser Wilhelm of Germany and Queen Wilhelmina of the Netherlands honored her for her musical achievements. After the outbreak of World War I she returned to the United States, married an Albert Lea physician, and managed music conservatories there and in Minneapolis. Bessesen saw music as the art that most successfully transcended national boundaries. The flight of French aviators Dieudonné Coste and Maurice Bellonte from Paris to New York in 1930 inspired her to write the following statement:

> When Coste and [Bellonte] were here, our own hearts responded to the [Marseillaise], and when the Star-Spangled Banner was played in France for our hero Lindbergh, I am sure the French people felt the same way, for music with its harmonies of voice and instruments and melodies is the golden thread that can weave a beautiful friendship among nations. Soul speaks to Soul in music, and it appeals essentially to the emotions.

CERAMIC ARTIST

Henrietta Barclay Paist was born in Red Wing in 1870. She studied ceramics in Germany, watercolor painting in Minneapolis, and design in Chicago before spending the remainder of her career in the Twin Cities as an artist and painter of portraits and miniatures on china and traditional canvas.

CHAPTER X.

SHAKSPERE INCAPABLE OF WRITING THE PLAYS.

A very superficial, ignorant, unweighing fellow.
Measure for Measure, iii. 2.

EVERY *Cipher word in this chapter also is the 327th word from the same points of departure which have given us all the Cipher story which has preceded it.*

We have this further statement from Cecil to the Queen:

516	349	327	327
167 (74:2)	22 b & h	50	30
349	327	277	297

	Word.	Page and Column.	
516—167—349—22 b & h—327—50—277—50—227.			
603—227—376+1—377.	377	76:2	He
516—167—349—22 b & h—327—30—297—193—104.	104	74:1	is
516—167—349—22 b & h—327—30—297—193—104—			
50—54—50 (76:1)—4. 508—4—504+1—505+1 h—506	506	75:2	the
516—167—349—22 b & h—327—30—297—193—	104	75:2	son
516—167—349—22 b & h—327—30—297—193—104—			
15 b & h—89. 448—89—359+1—360.	360	76:1	of
516—167—349—22 b & h—327—50—277—50 (76:1)—	227	76:2	a
516—167—349—22 b & h—327—49 (76:2)—85.	85	75:1	poor
516—167—349—22 b & h—327—146 (76:2)—181—			
9 h & b—(172).	(172)	75:2	peasant
516—167—349—22 b & h—327—30—297—49 (76:1)—			
248—248—0+1—1.	1	74:2	who
516—167—349—22 b & h—327—50—277—146—131.	131	76:1	yet
516—167—349—22 b & h—327—30—297—193—104.			
448—104—344+1—345.	345	76:1	followed
516—167—349—22 b & h—327—50—277—145—132			
10 b—122.	122	74:1	the
516—167—349—22 b & h—327—193—134—5 h (193)			
—129—2 h—127.	127	76:1	trade
516—167—349—22 b & h—327—50—277—193—84—			
15 b & h—69—10 b—59.	59	74:1	of
516—167—349—22 b & h—327—30—297—193—104—			
15 b & h—89. 508—89—419+1—420.	420	75:2	glove
516—167—349—22 b & h—327—50—277. 284—277—			
7+1—8+18 b & h—(26).	(26)	74:1	making

729

DONNELLY'S CRYPTOGRAM

Ignatius Donnelly, a gifted nineteenth-century politician, also ranked among Minnesota's best-known novelists and literary critics of the era. In *The Great Cryptogram* (1887), Donnelly argued that Sir Francis Bacon and not William Shakespeare had written such plays as *Hamlet*, *Romeo and Juliet*, and *King Lear*. His proof was an intricately ciphered code that he had detected in the text of the plays. The book attracted few buyers and fewer believers, but it did earn Donnelly a trip to England for debates at Oxford and Cambridge universities. Donnelly's own heavily annotated copy of the book indicates that his work on the cipher did not end with publication.

NORTHLAND AUTHOR

Walter O'Meara wrote about the north country in *The Trees Went Forth, The Savage Country*, and other novels.

FAMILY CENSUS

Census enumerators made it to the Redwood County home of Charles and Caroline Ingalls in 1875, long before their daughter Laura Ingalls Wilder wrote her acclaimed *Little House on the Prairie* books.

RESTLESS SPIRITS

Frank Bigbear, an Ojibway artist who grew up on White Earth Reservation and now lives in Minneapolis, explores his personal experiences in brilliant colored-pencil drawings that are inspired by his tribal heritage as well as big-city life. *Restless Spirits* combines the colors and patterns of Ojibway beadwork with the equally vivid effects of contemporary art.

A Capitol Place

SERIES OF TWENTY DIFFERENT STAMPS SENT FOR 10¢

MINNESOTA STATE CAPITOL
SAINT PAUL

ISSUED UNDER DIRECTION OF ST. PAUL ASSOCIATION OF COMMERCE

POLITICS ABLAZE WITH PASSION

Politics has been a flammable topic in Minnesota from the start. The state has raised suffragists and socialists, populists and prohibitionists, rightists and racists, anarchists and agricultural radicals — truly a combustible combination of political convictions.

It is not surprising, then, that Minnesota's first Capitol building, a brick structure built in 1853 at the corner of Tenth and Cedar streets in St. Paul, collapsed in an impressive inferno after twenty-eight years of service. As legislators moved their offices into temporary quarters, workers cleared the charred rubble from the site and raised a new building on the same spot.

The second Capitol better withstood the heat of Minnesota politics, but it could not keep up with the mushrooming growth of population and governmental services. The governor, state civil servants, and legislators needed more space. In 1893 a state commission began to search for a site for a new building and for an architect to design it. The commissioners selected a rise north of downtown St. Paul as the site and chose young Cass Gilbert as the architect.

Gilbert, a native of Ohio who had been a practicing architect in St. Paul for several years, ranked among the state's most gifted building planners. In later years he made a specialty of designing skyscrapers, including the famous Woolworth Building in New York City, which at the time of its erection in 1913 was the world's tallest. He also designed the U.S. Supreme Court Building in Washington, D.C.

For the Minnesota Capitol, Gilbert created a majestic — critics called it pretentious — plan. Inspired by the architecture of the Italian High Renaissance, he designed a frontal plaza featuring steps and terraces. The plan for the building itself called for Corinthian columns, arched entrances, and two end pavilions. Rock from Minnesota quarries would dress the building. As the highlight, Gilbert created a huge central dome modeled after the one Michelangelo had designed for St. Peter's Basilica in Rome.

Gilbert also concerned himself with the furnishings of the new building. He designed chairs, tables, desks, wardrobes, bookcases, and sofas and commissioned furniture manufacturers around the country to build them. Over the decades the state moved, sold, or destroyed hundreds of pieces of original Capitol furnishings, and it was not until 1989 that about eight hundred items were at last located and cataloged.

The building was completed in 1905. Sixty-four years later the state acknowledged another facet of the building's importance, in addition to its role as the seat of government. In 1969 the Capitol was designated a state historic site. Minnesotans formally recognized the significance of the state's fiery political past while anticipating the burning issues, debates, elections, and decisions yet to come.

◄

CAMPAIGN BUTTONS
Political ephemera — in other words, the bumper stickers, buttons, and badges that announce our enthusiasm for one candidate or another in national, state, and local contests. This selection is a bare sampling of the countless campaign items that Minnesotans have displayed since statehood.

CAPITOL MISCELLANY
A plaster model, details from two Capitol chairs, and a tiny souvenir vase from the early 1900s. The chair with the rectangular back was brought to the new Capitol from the former building; the other one was designed by Cass Gilbert.

GILBERT DRAWING

Cass Gilbert was one of Minnesota's brightest young architects in the mid-1890s when he prepared the design for the third Capitol building. This linen drawing is an early rendering of his proposal for the south front elevation. The sterling silver trowel was presented to Alexander Ramsey, the former governor, when the cornerstone was laid on July 27, 1898.

CAPITOL CONSTRUCTION

Rock for the Capitol (top) was quarried at Mankato, Ortonville, St. Cloud, and Winona. The photo below shows the Capitol building with the side walls in place, about 1900.

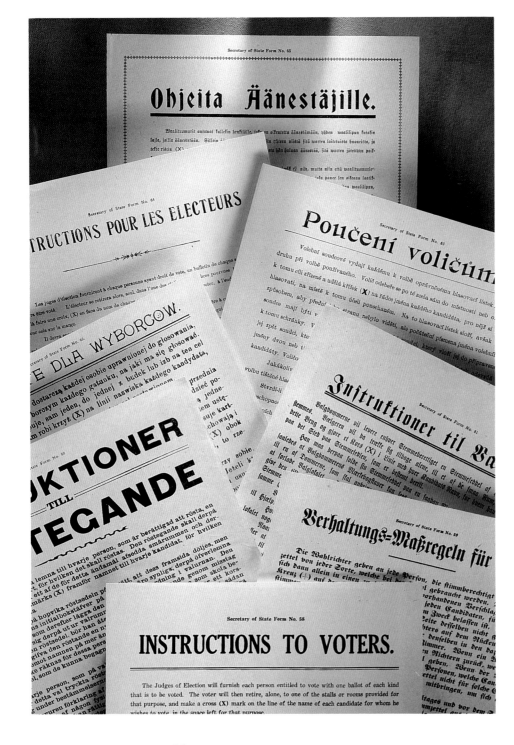

RECOUNTING THE VOTES

The 1962 gubernatorial race between Democratic-Farmer-Labor candidate Karl F. Rolvaag and Republican incumbent Elmer L. Andersen was the closest election in state history. During the weeks required for a recount, Andersen remained in the governor's office while Rolvaag occupied an office in the basement of the Capitol. The final tally confirmed Rolvaag's victory, 619,842 to 619,751. These two recount documents are from Douglas County. ▶

VOTING INSTRUCTIONS

The high number of first-generation immigrants in the early decades of the twentieth century prompted Minnesota officials to issue voting instructions in many languages. Those shown here in (from top) Finnish, French, Czech, Polish, Norwegian, Swedish, German, and English were issued between 1928 and 1936.

DOMESTIC SERVICE
Check the class of service desired, otherwise this message will be sent as a fast telegram
TELEGRAM
DAY LETTER
NIGHT LETTER

INTERNATIONAL SERVICE
Check the class of service desired, otherwise the message will be sent at the full rate
FULL RATE
LETTER TELEGRAM
SHORE SHIP

WESTERN UNION
TELEGRAM
W. P. MARSHALL, PRESIDENT

1207 (4-55)

NO. WDS-CL. OF SVC | PD. OR COLL. | CASH NO. | CHARGE TO THE ACCOUNT OF | TIME FILED

Send the following message, subject to the terms on back hereof, which are hereby agreed to

To ___ GOVERNOR ELMER L. ANDERSON ___ Nov. 14 __ 1962

Street and No. ___ State Capitol
Care of or
Apt. No. ___ Destination ___ St. Paul, Minnesota

Douglas County Board of Canvass will reconvene
November 16, 2 P.M. to recount Alexandria Fifth
Ward for office of Governor.

R. I. Pennar
County Auditor

Sender's name and address (For reference)   Sender's telephone number

35

---

telegram to each of the candidates read as follows:

"Douglas County Board of Canvass will reconvene November 16, 2 P.M. to recount Alexandria Fifth Ward for office of Governor.

R. I. Pennar
County Auditor"

That attached to the original of these minutes and made a part hereof are copies of the telegram sent to the candidates, together with proof of service thereof.

Mr. Pennar also stated that he had notified by telephone Willard Olson, Douglas County Chairman of the Democratic Farmer Labor party, and Carl Dahlin, Douglas County Chairman of the Republican party.

The Canvassing Board then proceeded to inspect and re-examine the ballots and the returns of the Fifth Ward of the City of Alexandria with the following results:

Registered voters	Anderson	Rolvaag
919	644	271

The Canvassing Board then proceeding to inspect and re-examine the ballots and the returns of Alexandria Township with the following results:

Registered voters	Anderson	Rolvaag
715	392	311

The County Auditor was directed to immediately notify the Secretary of State of the change of results in the vote for Governor in the precincts involved, by furnishing to the Secretary of State copies of these minutes, all in accordance with Sec. 204.30 Minn. Statutes.

Kenneth Cverdell County Commissioner, Fifth District
A. B. Myren County Commissioner, Third District
R. Pennar County Auditor
E. Smith Clerk of District Court
Marcus Hansen Mayor of the City of Alexandria

33

"SHOULD I MAKE THE ATTEMPT?"

In January 1972, when a federal court rearranged Minnesota's legislative districts, aspiring Bloomington politician Ray Pleasant discovered that he lived just one block inside a new house district that included parts of Bloomington, Eden Prairie, and Edina. He recorded his reaction in his diary:

> Now, the question is — "Should I make the attempt to run for that seat in the House of Representatives?"
>
> What will be the [effect] upon my family? Will I have more time with them or even less than I do at the present time?
>
> Will Viitalla (former councilman) called and stated that every thing is set "for you to go. You are Mr. '27C.' We have to get together with Otto Bang — he is running for the Senate seat. We will get you elected as the first Black to the legislature."
>
> "You are [too] late by several years."
>
> "That right!?! Well at any rate I need you over there to hold the *budget* down."

Pleasant ran for the seat in 1972 and won the election.

THE MEETING

Many workers banded together to seek political and social change during the Great Depression. Artist Syd Fossum was both observer and participant in gatherings of groups like the Workers' Alliance, the subject of this 1937 oil painting, which includes portraits of Fossum's friends and fellow activists.

I MARRIED A POLITICIAN

If the public's expectations of political officeholders are demanding, so are the stresses placed on the politician's family. As part of a continuing series of oral history interviews with the spouses of Minnesota governors, Gretchen Quie, wife of Governor Albert H. Quie, described the abrupt changes she felt once her husband assumed office in 1978:

> The wife of a politician who moves into [the governor's mansion] probably never had that kind of experience before, and you come out of your own ordinary home – there are a few people who come from very wealthy families and have backgrounds of servants and schedules and all these things, but most of us are very middle class citizens who suddenly are living in a grand house that belonged to millionaires. . . . I had never hired anyone but a once a week cleaning lady before, and suddenly here you are trying to be part of the direction for 7–8 people on the staff and getting used to security men, and all these little things [that] there is no way to train for. . . .

> Some days I woke up so early in the morning just wondering how in the world that day was going to go, or . . . some big event. And most things went quite smoothly, you know, [but] every once in awhile there was a lot of tension maybe with some staff, or some decision on how an event should be arranged. . . . To the public, it looked great but, you know, behind the scenes we knew that there were things that have been a big problem.

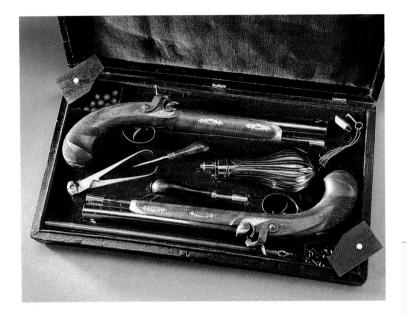

DUELING PISTOLS

Although Alexander Ramsey may have had fleeting thoughts about resorting to firepower to deal with contentious politicians, he did not himself purchase this ornate set of dueling pistols. They came to him in 1864 as a gift from Calhoun Deringer, who studied at Ramsey's alma mater, Lafayette College in Pennsylvania.

THE BURDENS OF OFFICE

The constant pull and shove, struggle and compromise, and interparty conflict of government can wear down politicians and constituents alike. In 1851, while territorial governor, Alexander Ramsey described to his friend Henry H. Sibley his ambivalent feelings about leading Minnesota's government:

> [A]s for this office the slightest cause will induce me to return
> it to the Pres[iden]t: in truth I am beginning to be tired of it,
> it has ceased to be a novelty. . . . [A] man who remains in
> place must despise himself.

Six years later Sibley narrowly defeated Ramsey to become the first governor of the State of Minnesota. Ramsey attained the same office in 1860, and he later served as a United States senator and then secretary of war in the cabinet of President Rutherford B. Hayes. He died in 1903.

PHOTOGRAPHS

Jerome Liebling, one of the state's greatest fine art photographers, supplemented his teaching income by taking pictures for the *Minnesota Legislative Manual* in the 1960s. One of his artworks, *DFL Rally, 1958*, is shown here alongside the manual and a photo that appeared in it.

STICKING TO HIS PRINCIPLES

Things are constantly in a state of revision and rethinking in politics. Hubert H. Humphrey was renowned for revising his speeches as he spoke. In 1948 Humphrey was in the middle of his first campaign to win election as a United States senator from Minnesota. He took advantage of an unusual opportunity to gain a national audience during the Democratic National Convention that summer, when he spoke before the assembled delegates in support of a strong civil-rights platform. His eloquent eight-minute speech so impressed the delegates that they voted against the leadership and approved the measure, which had been overwhelmingly defeated the day before by the platform committee. Here is the text of a section of the final draft of Humphrey's speech:

> We cannot use a double standard for measuring our own and other people's policies. Our demands for democratic practices in other lands will be no more effective than the guarantee of those practices is in our own country.
>
> We are God-fearing men and women. We place our faith in the brotherhood of man under the fatherhood of God.
>
> I do not believe that there can be any compromise on the guarantee of civil rights which I have mentioned. In spite of my desire for unanimous agreement on the platform, there are some matters which I think must be stated without qualification. There can be no hedging—no watering down.

But here is what Humphrey actually said when he faced the Democratic delegates:

> We cannot use a double standard. There's no room for double standards in American politics, for measuring our own and other people's policies. Our demands for democratic practices in other lands will be no more effective than the guarantee of those practices in our own country.
>
> Friends, delegates—I do not believe that there can be any compromise on the guarantees of the civil rights which we have mentioned in the minority report. In spite of my desire for unanimous agreement on the entire platform, in spite of my desire to see everybody here in unanimous agreement, there are some matters which I think must be stated clearly and without qualification. There can be no hedging. The newspapers are wrong. There will be no hedging—no watering down—of the instruments and the principles of the civil rights program.

WOMAN SUFFRAGE

Harriet E. Bishop, Jane Grey Swiss-helm, Martha G. Ripley, Clara Hampson Ueland, and many other Minnesota women fought for woman suffrage from the mid-nineteenth century through 1920, when the Nineteenth Amendment to the U.S. Constitution gave women full voting rights. Even so, women in Minnesota had only won the right to vote in local school and library board elections before the amendment became law.

DEAR SENATOR

Minnesota's elected officials receive thousands of letters every year. Many constituents wrote during the Vietnam War to express their feelings and political viewpoints. Within four days in January 1967, Senator Eugene J. McCarthy received these two letters:

Dear Senator:

How long must this Vietnam war go on? Boys being laid to rest every day by the score. Boys who pray to live and hate to die. Mothers grieving who have worked so hard to raise them.

Why are we giving so much goodies to the enemy that is hurting us so?

Why don't we give the North Vietnam Government 48 hours to come to the conference table or we will really bomb every thing, then give them 24 hours to surrender or hit them again. . . .

I bet some of the past Presidents would roll over in [their] graves at some of the things that are going on now. Am I not right?

Dear Senator McCarthy;

I have a weak and puny voice[,] am somewhat of a coward, and an expert at procrastinating. But if I am to live with myself that weak and puny voice must speak. . . .

It's the war in Vietnam. We are destroying what we supposedly set out to save. All of our efforts seem to lack direction. . . . We endeavor to educate our youth, then brain wash them into becoming good soldiers. And they are good, they care for and love the children whose parents they have killed and whose homes they have burned.

. . . How can we protect the poor innocents with guns. We can't even tell them in their own language what we are about. Nor can they tell us. Couldn't we show them our love with food & more food.

War Front, Home Front

See America First Series 8 Glacier Nat'l Park

DEPARTMENT OF WAR
LINDLEY MILLER GARRISON

All swords turned into plowshares in the
Zone of Plenty along the Great Northern Ry.

© B.& B ST P

THE MARCH TO WAR

Early on the morning of April 14, 1861, Governor Alexander Ramsey of Minnesota rushed up the steps to the office of U.S. Secretary of War Simon Cameron. By chance, Ramsey — a Republican — was in Washington, D.C., seeking political jobs for his campaign workers when he heard the somber news that forces of the Confederate states had fired upon the Union garrison at Fort Sumter, South Carolina. Even worse, Fort Sumter had raised the white flag.

Ramsey gave Cameron a written offer of one thousand Minnesota troops to join the Union armies. The secretary later delivered this offer to President Abraham Lincoln, making Minnesota the first northern state to volunteer soldiers in the Civil War.

In making the offer, Ramsey was taking a calculated risk. The state had about 26,000 men eligible for service, but only 347 officers and enlisted men were registered in the militia. Would hundreds more volunteer to fight in a war raging so far from home?

They did. Within less than three weeks, nine hundred members of the First Minnesota Infantry Volunteer Regiment were at Fort Snelling, awaiting orders. The commanding officer of the group, former Minnesota territorial governor Willis A. Gorman, was a veteran of the Mexican War, but his two highest-ranking subordinates had never before served in the military.

The most pressing task of the regiment was to learn how to drill. Officers paged through tactical manuals and ran the recruits through daylong training. Citizens living near the fort treated the troops to parades and picnics, as well as donations of gear and other presents. Still, the soldiers were restless to move east.

Finally, orders came to travel to Washington. The fort rollicked with celebration, and St. Paulites organized a large parade through their city. In late June, more than two months after the southern assault on Fort Sumter, the men boarded steamboats and then trains bound for the capital.

It was not long before Minnesotans faced the realities of war. On July 21 the volunteers were sent into the Battle of Bull Run, where they performed creditably despite heavy casualties and the eventual victory of the Confederates. Meanwhile, as the war progressed, other Minnesota regiments filled their ranks with volunteers and drafted soldiers, with the total number of state residents in the Union army eventually reaching twenty-four thousand. These additional fighting groups participated in important Civil War battles at Corinth, Vicksburg, Chickamauga, Chattanooga, and Nashville.

Back at home Minnesotans endured the much-feared dispatches of casualty lists and the absence of thousands of able-bodied young men. In the summer of 1862 the U.S.–Dakota Conflict brought tragedy to white settlers and Indians alike. At the same time, women ran businesses and farms while gathering clothing, food, and medical supplies for the soldiers. Both Republicans and Democrats supported President Lincoln's policies; the Democrats, however, tended to justify the hostilities as necessary to preserve the Union, whereas the Republicans more often believed that the abolition of slavery was also an aim of the Union effort.

On the battlefield it was the First Minnesota Volunteers who played a crucial role in perhaps the most legendary engagement of the war. Now under the command of William Colvill, a journalist from Red Wing, the regiment received orders from General Winfield S. Hancock to charge the advancing southern lines on July 2, 1863, during the Battle of Gettysburg. Eight Minnesota companies halted the Confederate troops, but not without severe penalty: almost half of the volunteers were killed or wounded. Accompanied by two other Minnesota companies, the survivors rallied on the following day to turn back the southerners in a decisive second engagement.

Minnesota was in a deep winter freeze when the First Minnesota returned home to St. Paul on February 15, 1864, more than two and a half years after joyously heading east from Fort Snelling. A city holiday was declared, and five thousand cheering citizens met the returning soldiers. Wounded at Gettysburg, Colonel Colvill was carried by his fellow officers to his carriage for the parade through the city.

◄

WAR FRONT
A poster from World War I is shown against uniforms that Minnesotans wore in several of the nation's military conflicts. The U.S. Navy shirt at left was part of a dress blue uniform worn during the Korean War, and the leather flight jacket above it was worn by a WASP (Women's Air Force Service Pilot) during World War II. At top right is the jacket from a U.S. Army dress uniform worn by a serviceman who was killed in the Vietnam War. The olive-drab French uniform at bottom right was worn by a volunteer in an ambulance corps in France beginning in April 1917.

Muster rolls and an elegant presentation sword belonging to General John B. Sanford of St. Paul, who served in the Fourth Minnesota Infantry Volunteer Regiment, date from the Civil War. The newspaper is a special edition of the *St. Paul Pioneer Press* issued on May 8, 1915, to report the sinking of the British liner *Lusitania* by a German submarine.

SAMUEL BADGER, DRUMMER BOY

Samuel Badger was the drummer boy of Company H, Fourth Minnesota Infantry Volunteer Regiment. This pastel portrait, which is nearly life-size, was made by an unidentified artist.

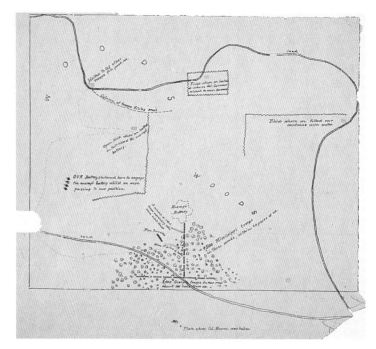

BATTLE MAP

Javan B. Irvine, a Civil War private from St. Paul, drew this map of the movements of the First Minnesota Infantry Volunteer Regiment at the First Battle of Bull Run, July 21, 1861. A few months after the battle Irvine was promoted, joining a regular unit as a lieutenant. He served as a career army officer until his retirement in 1891.

HOME FRONT

The demands of war can affect virtually every aspect of life back home. This apron was part of a costume used in a World War II campaign to encourage U.S. Postal Savings. The food that cooks prepared in their own kitchens was probably patriotic as well. Homemakers coped with rationing and shortages by using meat extenders like Cream of Rye—represented here by recipes from World War I.

The government used posters to exhort citizens to cooperate with the war effort, and the decision to volunteer as an air raid warden or to contribute to war relief overseas was a response to that call. During all wars, some citizens have chosen to challenge the use of military force as a way to resolve conflict. Those beliefs are reflected here in antiwar buttons from the Vietnam era.

GOLD STAR

After World War I the families of those who had died in the war were encouraged to apply for commemorative Gold Star status. The applications, which were processed by the Minnesota Commission of Public Safety in cooperation with the Minnesota War Records Commission, often included photographs, letters, and newspaper clippings about the person who had died. Two decades later the Gold Star tradition was continued during World War II: the flag shown here was bestowed on the family of Leland Rollag Rowberg, a serviceman from Northfield who was killed in action near Metz, Germany, in October 1944.

SHIP'S WHEEL

The wheel of the USS *Minnesota*, which played a role in one of the world's most important naval battles. On March 8, 1862, wooden-sided Union ships at anchor in Hampton Roads, Virginia, were attacked by the *Merrimack*, a captured northern vessel that the Confederates had innovatively sided with iron. The *Merrimack* badly damaged the Union ships. On the following day the *Merrimack* returned and was about to fire upon the *Minnesota* when an odd-looking Union ship came to the rescue: the *Monitor*. It, too, had metal sides and resembled a floating box. The two ironclad ships battled for more than three hours. Finally the vessels parted, neither the decisive victor. No one doubted, however, that the days of the wooden-clad ships were numbered.

PILLOW COVER

A souvenir Fort Snelling pillow cover dating from the 1940s, shown with holiday menus from the Minnesota Soldiers' Home.

From 1820 through World War II, the fort – first called Fort St. Anthony – at the confluence of the Minnesota and Mississippi rivers played a leading role in the region's military history. Founded as a remote frontier outpost, it once included a vast reservation extending over what is now much of the Twin Cities metropolitan area. Although never the scene of a battle, it guarded the northwest fur trade, was the training camp of soldiers bound for the Civil War, quartered hundreds of Dakota people after the 1862 conflict, and again served as a training center during the two world wars. A restoration completed in 1979 returned it to the way it appeared in the mid-1820s.

A LETTER FROM THE FRONT

On December 11, 1864, Leonard Aldrich, a Civil War officer with the Eighth Minnesota regiment in Tennessee, wrote home to his brother and sister about the hardship and horror he had encountered in the fighting. "It is a cold blustering day," he began. "The ground is covered with snow and ice making it very bad for the soldiers who have no protection but those little shelter tents."

Aldrich described an attack that his regiment and others had staged on the Confederates:

> The line just commenced to move forward. We were in exact range of the enemies cannon. They opened fire. The first ball struck the ground not more than 4 feet in front of me and bounded over the next company on my right. The second ball struck the center of my company killing Mr. Higgins and Mr. Payton and wounding Walter Strathern.

At one point, with senior officers unavailable, Aldrich assumed command:

> I ordered an other charge. The whole regiment went with a rush and a yell. Drove the enemy from their fortifications and the woods. They left in disorder leaving their wounded and dead. We also took their cannon. Our regiment has got a good name. . . . I had three killed and sixteen wounded. Sergeant Brigham was killed. Lieut. Fowler wounded in right hand. Sergt. Couper in right shoulder. Corp. Millard in left side. Alonzo in left arm. George Coats in the head over right eye. Boyne in right shoulder. Elijah Houck in right thigh. S. Truesdell in right arm. The others were wounded slightly.

During a break in the fighting Aldrich visited a camp hospital:

> It is a sorrowful sight to go into the hospital and see the wounded, some with an arm off, and others with a leg. One man shot through the head, ball entering just above the right eye and coming out the back of the head. You can hardly imagine a place on the body where some poor fellow had not been hit. I don't think I heared a groan or a murmur from one of our regiment, no matter how severe the wound.

ALDRICH LETTER

A page from the letter describing the battle in Tennessee

We had a snug little engagement for about 2 hours, drove the enemy back, took several prisoners, only seven killed and nineteen wounded on our side, only one wounded in our regiment, that in co H. Skirmishing every day since, on Wednesday last, about ten regiments, six cannon, and nearly a regiment of cavalry, were ordered out to drive the enemy from their position which was well taken in heavy timber, were intrenched and fortified to a considerable extent. It took some time to find the place to make the attack. The cannonading commenced about 10 o'clock. About 2 P.M. the Gen. thought best to flank their left, we had accomplished the movement, formed a new line of battle, the 61st Ill. on the right, the 8th Minn next, the 181 Ohio next and so on. The line just commenced to move forward, we were in exact range of the enemies cannon, they opened fire, the first ball struck the ground not more than 4 feet in front of me, and bounded over the next company on my right, the second ball struck the center of my company killing Mr Higgins and Mr Payton and wounding Walter Strathern. Mr Elliotte, Sen, Noyes and Geo. Rice, order double quick, soon got too near for their big guns, but came in contact with bullets from their muskets, they were in the

CIVIL WAR ALBUM

Members of Minnesota regiments as photographed by Joel Whitney. These pictures were assembled into an album of Civil War portraits by collector Edward A. Bromley.

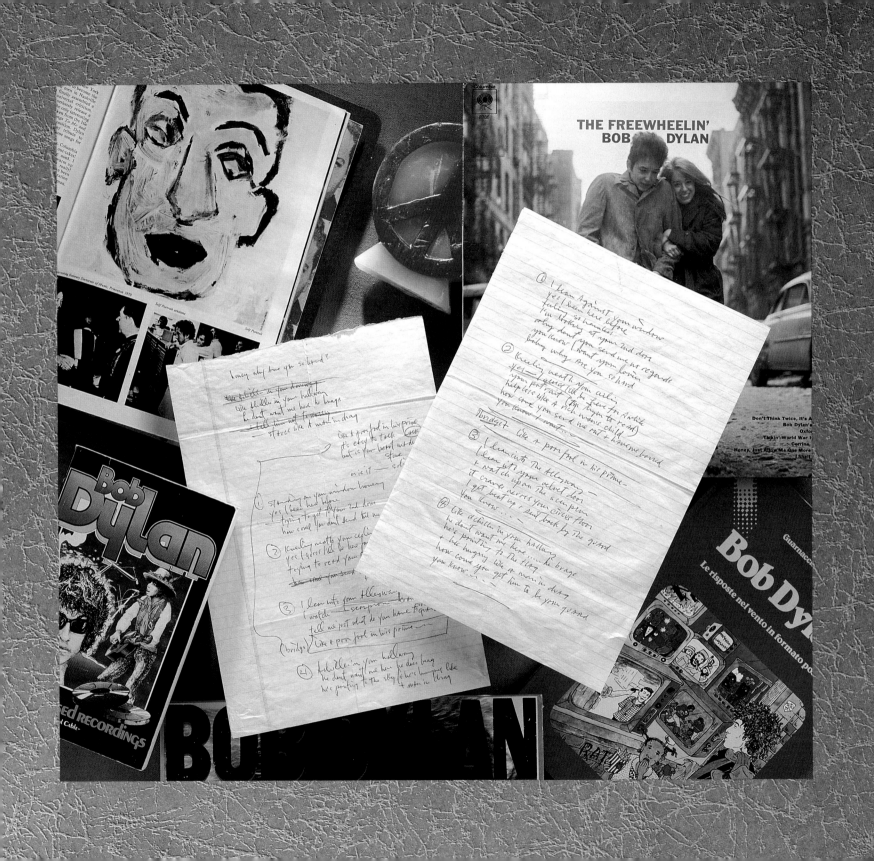

Growing Up

IT WAS A HAPPENING

What kind of place has Minnesota been to grow up in? There are as many answers to that question as there have been kids going through the experience.

And what was it like to grow up in Minnesota during the 1960s and early 1970s? Again, there is no easy answer. Political strife, racial conflict, and changes in the family structure emerged in Minnesota as elsewhere. Many young people took advantage of new freedoms in political expression, as well as in popular music and art, but not every kid rebelled or played a guitar or wrote poetry.

The words scattered below and on the following pages recall a time when coming of age meant listening to the Beatles or watching the *Mary Tyler Moore Show* on television. But childhood is also a timeless world, as reflected in things like paper dolls, high school souvenirs, toys, and clothing from many eras in Minnesota.

"The Mod Squad"

ten-speed bikes

Ali vs. Frazier

drug education films

Susie Homemaker

Billie Jean King

Amazon Bookstore

I can't believe I ate the whole thing

"Blowin' in the Wind"

Rosemary's Baby

one giant leap for mankind

Gus Hall

RED LAKE SCHOOL
A classroom at the elementary school
at Red Lake Reservation, about 1953

Tiny Tim

The Maltese Bippy

David Cassidy

Sly and the Family Stone

The Pueblo

◄

BOB DYLAN
Robert Zimmerman of Hibbing grew
into Bob Zimmerman, a student at the
University of Minnesota. Then, as Bob
Dylan, he played music in many
styles — including folk, rock, and born-
again gospel — for fans all over the
world. During a 1966 recording session
he wrote two versions of the song
"Temporary Like Achilles" for the
album *Blond on Blond.* He gave the
handwritten drafts to the recording
engineer, who later sold them to a
Nashville store. They are now part of
the Society's large collection of Dylan
records, books, and other materials.

Eugene Fodor

BOY'S VEST
Once the property of a Dakota child
who died at the age of seven in the late
nineteenth century, this vest is made
from native-tanned leather and beaded
porcupine quills. The striking lizard
figures attached to the back are amulets
carrying special meaning for the boy
to whom the vest belonged.

"Classical Gas"

Adam West

hawks and doves

troll dolls

Paul is dead

"Philadelphia Freedom"

PAPER DOLLS

A selection of paper dolls ranging from the antique to the contemporary. These figures and their wardrobes were manufactured between the 1860s and the 1940s.

COOTIE

For thirty-eight years beginning in 1948, Plymouth was the home of Schaper Manufacturing Company, best known to children as the maker of Cootie games. (The business was sold to New Jersey–based Tyco Toys in 1986.) In addition to Cooties—which William Schaper's original patent papers describe as a "separable toy figure"—the firm manufactured toy sporting equipment (hockey sticks and baseball bats) and such games and toys as Skunk, Stadium Checkers, Tickle Bee, Ants in Your Pants, and Stomper Monsters. And how did the name Cootie originate? According to Schaper, it is what U.S. troops called lice during World War I.

maxi-skirts

Gumby
afros

Lester Maddox

TRUCK

A classic Tonka dump truck, made in about 1965

plastic erasers

Kansas City 23, Vikings 7

The Unbelievable Uglies

Ravi Shankar

the metric system

Gregory Dee and the Avanties

Thomas Eagleton

Harold and Maude

K-Tel

Seven Corners

Jim Perry

love-ins

STUDENT NEWSPAPER
A page from a Lyon County high school newspaper

The Boston Strangler

GETTING AN EDUCATION

When migrant agricultural workers — most of them Hispanic — began coming to Minnesota in substantial numbers at the start of the twentieth century, their children often arrived with them. School districts in the state had an obligation to enroll the children and to keep track of their attendance.

School District No. 241 in Freeborn County maintained records of the 102 migrant children it enrolled during the 1967–68 school year. Many of the children attended for only a portion of the year — as few as eleven days. Here are the first ten names entered on the report, with the surnames abbreviated to protect the privacy of the students:

Name of pupil	Grade	Age	Days absent	Days present
Janie H.	2	7	0	26
Johnny R.	2	8	0	20
Andres R.	2	7	1	36
Esther R.	2	9	0	37
Eduardo R.	2	10	12½	39½
Ermalinda R.	2	9	1	10
Frank Y.	2	9	0	17
Teddy C.	3	8	12	6
Ernesto G.	3	9	1	16
Juanita G.	3	9	0	18

The Minnesota Seven

Linus Pauling

HIGH SCHOOL GRADUATION
St. Cloud State Reformatory, a correctional facility for juveniles, has operated educational programs during much of its history. Like any high school, it holds commencement ceremonies for its graduating students. This program is from 1966. Note the presence of a Minnesota Supreme Court associate justice as the commencement speaker.

Ken

Diahann Carroll

Island of the Blue Dolphins

WINNERS
Exhibiting a prize pet, as recorded (top) by Ricardo Block at the Sherburne County Fair, 1983, and by Paul Hamilton at the Minnesota State Fair, 1926

Pat Paulsen

Excelsior Amusement Park

hot pants

Peter Max

CLASS PIN
Members of the 1899 graduating class at Central High School, St. Paul, wore this distinctive fleur-de-lis pin.

Doug Head

Tonka trucks

Sounds Like Us

Attica

happenings

Mary, Murray, Georgette, Ted, and Mr. Grant

Zero Population Growth

GIRL SCOUT UNIFORM

Ethel Mae Bishop was seventeen and had earned twenty-five merit badges when she wore this uniform in the mid-1920s. Her troop met in St. Paul.

UFOs

Meathead

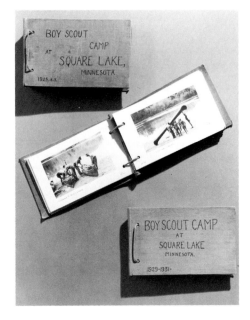

Lt. Uhura

Bud Grant

identical cousins

FUTURE FARMERS

Between 1963 and 1969 the Minnesota chapter of Future Farmers of America sponsored a program that gave young people experience in raising mallard ducklings for release in the wild. With the dual aims of education and of increasing the number of wildfowl in the state, the program involved more than 1,800 members of 161 FFA chapters in all corners of Minnesota. Of the 54,261 ducklings raised by the youngsters and released into the wild, 83 percent successfully survived in their new environment.

BOY SCOUT CAMP

Between 1902 and 1931 John W. G. Dunn photographed his three sons and later his Boy Scout campers growing up in St. Paul and the St. Croix River valley. Twenty albums of excellent snapshots and meticulous captions give one man's perceptions of boyhood in Minnesota.

"The Partridge Family"

Twiggy

Shirley Chisholm

ON THE PHONE
The beanbag chair: an essential kids' bedroom furnishing of the late 1960s and early 1970s. It was the next best thing to lying on the floor when you talked on your Princess telephone – a wildly popular convenience for the era's teenage girls. The houndstooth check jumper was part of the uniform at St. Paul Academy and Summit School in the 1970s.

Donald Duck in Mathimagic Land

G.I. Joe

grok

TOP
A thirteen-year-old Hmong immigrant boy in St. Paul fashioned this top out of simple materials: whittled wood, wool yarn, and a tree twig.

HAPPY BIRTHDAY
Buzza Craftacres, a Minneapolis company active between the 1910s and the 1930s, made cards to add sparkle to the birthdays of kids of all ages.

Bobby Seale

Wounded Knee

Good Sports

INDOOR PLAY/OUTDOOR PLAY

The big sporting debate in Minnesota during the late 1970s and early 1980s was not who could swing hardest, pass farthest, skate fastest, or dribble smoothest. It had nothing to do with teams or talent. It had everything to do with sky and ceiling.

On one side of the debate were the business interests of Minneapolis, joined by the management of the state's two most successful professional sports franchises: the Twins and the Vikings. They wanted a big new stadium built in downtown Minneapolis—a domed stadium. On the other side were the less powerful business interests of Bloomington (home of Met Stadium, which would end up bulldozed), augmented by a somewhat disorganized battalion of sports fans. Armed with a fondness for parking-lot tailgating, an indifference to frostbite, and a hurriedly generated nostalgia for the old stadium, this group wanted major-league baseball and football to remain where they had been played in the Twin Cities for the previous two decades.

Minnesotans uninterested in sports (a tiny fraction of the population, according to surveys) fell into neither camp, and to them the debate seemed senseless. A few pointed out that hundreds of millions of people each year watched traditionally outdoor major-league baseball and football on television from the indoor comfort of their living rooms. And, indeed, once the Hubert H. Humphrey Metrodome opened in downtown Minneapolis in 1982, its operators did their best to duplicate the living-room experience. A mammoth-screen TV set displayed instant replays (followed by bank and hardware store commercials), *Jeopardy*-like quizzes punctuated the innings and quarters, the air met household standards of healthfulness ("There is nooooooooooo smoking in the Metrodome! No smoking!"), and the only greenery on the field came from plastic plant life.

More germane to the futility of the debate, however, is Minnesota's historical embrace of both indoor and outdoor sports. Just as some athletes thumb their noses at the severe winters by skiing, skating, ice sailing, and broomballing with abandon, many others retreat to indoor tennis courts, basketball courts, racquetball courts, pools, batting cages, and running tracks. The first springlike day of the year provides either a liberation from the deep freeze or a continuation of outdoor activity, depending on one's fondness for cold weather.

Long before players like Kirby Puckett, Kent Hrbek, Frank Viola, and Gary Gaetti brought Minnesota its first World Series championship in 1987, baseball and softball reigned as the state's top outdoor sports. As early as 1884 major-league baseball arrived in the form of a pathetic St. Paul team, a member of the financially unstable Union Association league, that disbanded after playing only eight games — six of them losses. No other American major-league team, before or since, had such a short existence.

The intense rivalry between the Minneapolis Millers and the St. Paul Saints, minor-league clubs from the end of the nineteenth century through the arrival of the Twins, lasted for decades. So, too, has the influence of Lewis Rober, a Minneapolis firefighter who invented the game of outdoor softball in 1895, wrote its first book of rules, and is enshrined in the Softball Hall of Fame.

As in every other part of the country, the popularity of baseball changed outdoor recreation in Minnesota. Its arcane rules became known to virtually all boys — and in more recent decades, girls. Teams made up of American Indian and black players, both local and from outside Minnesota, toured the state, and minor-league teams brought pride to several towns.

But ever since they first donned the TC-emblazoned caps in 1961, it was the former Washington Senators, now the Twins, who symbolized the spirited use of bat and ball in Minnesota. In their fifth season of play the Twins won the American League championship, only to wither in the World Series before the Dodgers' Sandy Koufax and his fastball. Divisional championships followed in 1969 and 1970, but other teams swept past the Twins into the World Series.

A long seventeen seasons later, with a repeat performance in 1991, the Twins went all the way to the winner's circle. Kent Hrbek and Gene Larkin, respectively, slugged dramatic, game-winning hits in the 1987 and 1991 World Series, hammering nails in the coffins of their National League opponents as the crowds set records for deafening noise levels. And it all happened indoors.

◄

CURLING CLUBS
Minnesota is a hotbed of curling activity. Curling arrived from Scotland, where it is an important winter sport. Players slide forty-pound stones across the ice toward a circular goal (the house) and receive points for landing their stones within it. A curling tournament is called a bonspiel.

VIKINGS SWORD
Some football fans might complain that when it comes to getting a cut of Superbowl honors, the Minnesota Vikings might as well have been making their stabs with this souvenir inflatable sword. Since their first season in 1961 (the same year the Twins began playing in Minnesota), the Vikings have made it to Super Sunday four times — with nary a victory in the end.

```
IWINS WORLD CHAMPS


        LUNDS
   GOOD THINGS TO EAT
     62 ND AND PENN
       THANK YOU


  STORE#3      11/06/87


  CHEERIOS         1.57D
  SPRING WATER     2.21E
  PRODCE           1.99D
  ORANGE JUICE     2.99D
  GRAPE JUICE      1.79D
  QT 2% MILK        .59D
  D.H.COT.CH.       .49D
  STFR CHC PIE     1.65D
  CHIC NOODLES     1.95D
  HEALTH NUT B     1.19D
  CHARMIN           .99A
  MELITTA FLTR     1.57A
  1# WILD RICE     2.49D
  1# WILD RICE     2.49D
  NATUR SNACKS      .95D
     486   .33LB
       1LB/ 2.89
  BURITO            .83D
  BURITO            .83D
  3 MIN NOODLE      .25D
  3 MIN NOODLE      .25D
  3 MIN NOODLE      .25D
  RAMEN PRIDE       .25D
  ERROR
  RAMEN PRIDE      -.25D
  BURRITO           .49D
  TAX 1             .29H


       TOTAL     28.10

       CHECK     28.10

       CHANGE      .00

    3039 310 6  1.30PM
```

GROCERY RECEIPT

Shoppers at the check-out counter received the good news about the Twins' World Series victory in 1987.

WORLD SERIES

In a contest widely acclaimed as one of the best matched in baseball history, the Twins snatched a World Series victory from the Atlanta Braves in 1991.

The outside of the Metrodome was the site of face-offs as well, between Braves fans in American Indian regalia and Indian activists who protested the use of tomahawks, headdresses, and invented chants in team promotion.

SOFTBALL TEAM

The Intermediate Diamond Ball Team sponsored by the Phyllis Wheatley House in Minneapolis, 1926

TEAM PROGRAMS

The Twins, Vikings, Timberwolves, and North Stars by no means monopolize the state's professional and semi-professional sports history. Among the recent teams represented here are the Minnesota Fillies (women's basketball), Minnesota Muskies (men's basketball), Minnesota Fighting Saints (hockey), Minneapolis Lakers (basketball), Minnesota Pipers (basketball), Minneapolis Bruins (hockey), and Minnesota Norsemen (softball). Each has had its own diehard fans and moments of glory.

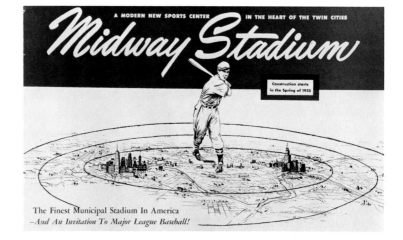

MIDWAY STADIUM

When St. Paul announced the start of construction for a new stadium near the State Fairgrounds in 1955, the city hoped that the ball park would one day be used by a major-league baseball team. But Bloomington won the competition to host the Minnesota Twins, and the Midway park never got the added second deck and increased seating capacity that this pamphlet envisioned. The stadium was torn down in 1981 to make way for Energy Park and was replaced at a nearby site by Municipal Stadium.

WALLY THE BEERMAN
METRODOME MINNEAPOLIS
1990

WALLY THE BEERMAN
Not every celebrity at the ball game
is a player.

TONI STONE
St. Paul native Toni Stone was the first
woman to play baseball professionally
when she signed with a team in the
Negro Leagues in 1949. Here she meets
boxer Joe Louis, about the same year.

WATER SKIS

One summer day in 1922 a Lake City teenager named Ralph Samuelson tried to keep his head above the water of Lake Pepin while wearing barrel staves on his feet and being towed by a noisy twenty-four-foot launch that was known locally as the "Roaring Bull." He failed. But after repeating the experiment wearing snowshoes and pine boards, Samuelson succeeded in inventing the sport of water skiing. His first pair of still-intact working skis, built that same summer, lasted until 1937 when a back injury forced Samuelson out of the sport. He did not receive official credit as the originator of water skiing until 1966.

HOCKEY

Minnesota's production of world-class hockey players is legendary, and the crack of stick meeting puck can be heard all over the state. This North Stars uniform is shown with souvenirs of hockey action in days past.

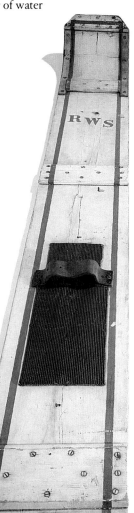
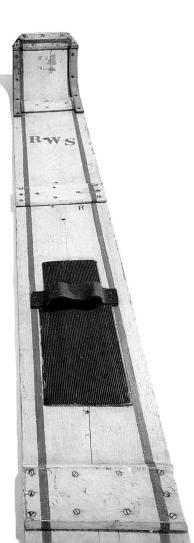

SCHOOL SPORTS

Although lacking the money and fancy equipment of professional sports, Minnesota's school athletics have long given fans thrills and young players glory. And school sports involve plenty of people besides the athletes: "Give me an A . . ."

◄

ON THE ICE

A century of ice skates in Minnesota, where people obviously love to glide. The oldest, the skates at bottom right with the acorn-tipped prow, were popular beginning in the 1830s. The pair at bottom left was the work of the Strauss family of St. Paul, makers of high-quality blades for a century.

America's first professional traveling ice show, the Ice Follies, was created by Minnesotans Eddie Shipstad and Oscar Johnson in 1936. Spectacular photographs and films show the Follies from their origins through the 1960s.

Contributors

Jack El-Hai is a Minneapolis writer with special interest in history, business, and the arts.

Staff members of the Minnesota Historical Society contributed generously of their time and knowledge to make this book possible. Coordinating these efforts were Marcia G. Anderson, curator of Museum Collections, who served as project manager; James E. Fogerty, head of the Acquisitions and Curatorial Department; and Elaine H. Carte, editor at the Minnesota Historical Society Press.

ACQUISITIONS AND CURATORIAL DEPARTMENT

Patrick K. Coleman, acquisitions librarian; Todd J. Daniels-Howell, associate curator of manuscript acquisitions; Mark A. Greene, curator of manuscript acquisitions; Thomas O'Sullivan, curator of art; Jon L. Walstrom, map curator; Bonnie G. Wilson, curator of sound and visual collections

STATE ARCHIVES DEPARTMENT

Mary P. Klauda, government records archivist; Charles L. Rodgers, government records archivist; Duane P. Swanson, acting head

MUSEUM COLLECTIONS DEPARTMENT

Nancy Bergh, collections cataloger; Patty Dean, collections manager; Charles O. Diesen, collections archaeologist; Kendra Dillard, curator of historic sites collections; Sherri Gebert Fuller, loan/research assistant; David Hermann, museum assistant; Linda McShannock, loan/research coordinator; Tracy Swanholm, collections access assistant; Jeff Tordoff, collections cataloger

MINNESOTA HISTORICAL SOCIETY PRESS

Jean A. Brookins, publisher; Nordis Heyerdahl-Fowler, marketing manager; Anne R. Kaplan, editor; Alan Ominsky, production supervisor; Ann Regan, managing editor

The following illustrations are reproduced by permission: *pages 3, 61, and 68,* portions of insurance maps of Sauk Centre, South St. Paul, and St. Paul, copyright 1929, 1939, and 1926 by Sanborn Mapping and Geographic Information Service, Pelham, N.Y.; *page 18,* illustration from *The Birds of Minnesota* by Thomas S. Roberts, copyright 1932, 1959, rev. 2d ed. copyright 1936, 1964, by the University of Minnesota Press, Minneapolis; *page 32,* portion of 1980 plat map, Rockford Map Publishers, Inc., Rockford, Ill.; *page 50,* High Bridge engravings, Gaylord Schanilec; *page 71,* Polk's St. Paul City Directory, 1929 and 1961, R. L. Polk & Co., Detroit, Mich.; *page 75,* page from *Millions of Cats* by Wanda Gág, copyright 1928 by Coward-McCann, Inc., New York, N.Y., renewed 1956 by Robert Janssen, reprinted by permission of Coward-McCann.

The colorful poster stamps appearing on the first pages of eleven of the twelve chapters were among thousands that Minnesota companies—eager to advertise their products and services—issued for collecting purposes, especially during the 1920s. The image on page 23 shows part of a parfleche bag, a decorated rawhide container that was probably made by a Blackfoot woman between 1880 and 1900.

COLOPHON

Staff photography by Phillip A. Hutchens

Photography of History Center (p. vi) and of artifacts by Eric Mortenson, with the following exceptions: p. 13, Daguerreotypes, Phillip A. Hutchens; p. 33, Threshing Machine, Thomas A. Woods; p. 103, Truck, Peter Latner

Book and cover design by Craig S. Davidson, CIVIC, Minneapolis

Composed in Janson and Gill Sans typefaces by Peregrine Publications, St. Paul

Color separations, printing, and binding by Friesen Printers, Altona, Manitoba